TRIM & TERRIFIC™

ONE-DISH FAVORITES

Over 200 Fast & Easy Low-Fat Recipes

TRIM & TERRIFIC™
ONE-DISH FAVORITES

Over 200 Fast & Easy Low-Fat Recipes

HOLLY BERKOWITZ CLEGG

Clarkson Potter/Publishers
New York

To my children, Todd, Courtney, and Haley,
for their enthusiasm, for always tasting my recipes, and
for being the best children a mom could ever have.
And, of course, to my devoted husband.

Published by Clarkson N. Potter, Inc., 201 East 50th Street, New York, New York 10022. Member of the Crown Publishing Group.

Random House, Inc. New York, Toronto, London, Sydney, Auckland
http://www.randomhouse.com/

CLARKSON N. POTTER, POTTER, and colophon are
trademarks of Clarkson N. Potter, Inc.

Trim & Terrific is a trademark of Holly Berkowitz Clegg.

Printed in the United States of America.

Design by Susan DeStaebler

Illustrations by Dick Cole

Library of Congress Cataloging-in-Publication Data is available upon request.

ISBN 0-517-70258-4

10 9 8 7 6 5 4 3 2 1

First Edition

Acknowledgments

I feel very fortunate that my hobby has turned into such a fun career. I want to thank all the special people in my life who are always there for me and give my life such balance. To my husband, Mike, who will always be number one in my life. Thank you for your patience, love, and encouragement. To Todd, who continually makes me so proud of his teenage years instead of wanting to forget them. To Courtney, who could probably run my family and my business as well as me. To Haley, my special little girl who is the spirit of our family. I love the hugs and kisses! To Mother and Daddy, who have spoiled me with love and continue to keep listening. To Mae Mae, for helping with the kids and making lots of roasts with rice and gravy. To Ilene and Bart, for being only a phone call away, hauling me around, and sharing it all! To Pam and Jim, for their continual promotion of my books and celebrating together always. To Michael and Kim, for spreading the word. To Nana and Papa, for doing whatever I need done and taping all those shows. My friends continue to be there for me . . . Francine, for being the best friend and sharing every aspect of my life and still being interested; Gail, you're my most caring taster and listener in my kitchen; Mary, for taking such good care of my kids and me; Louise, for a most cherished friendship and the best partner; Janet, for our telephone conversations and special bond; and my fun tennis friends: Lynell, Regina, Brenda, Carol, Monica, Kara, Penny, Dorraine, Jerry, and Carole. To Melanie, my creative confidante; Louann and Ronnie, for cooking, doctoring, and always being available. To Shirley, my number one help in the kitchen; Freddie, for my telephone talks; Lynda, for typing; Robin, for my beginning; Greg, for making all my numbers work. To my Newcomb College classmates—Sherri, Jolie, Lila, Leslie, and Lauren—for tasting all my creations in my toaster oven. My media pals: *NBC Weekend Today Show*, for including me in my favorite show. Jill Melton, for friendship and being a part of *Cooking Light*.

Nancy Gottesman, I love working with my L.A. connection for *Shape* and *Shape Cooks.* Jim Burns, all my freelance work with the *Los Angeles Times.* Mercantile: I love being your spokesperson, promoting your stores, and hope to make housewares an important part of everyone's lives. To Gene Winick, for being my guardian and including me in your family when I'm with you.

To the Clarkson Potter group: Katie, a most talented editor, but more important my dear friend. Thank you for preserving my voice throughout my book while adding your professionalism. Wendy, sharing each day of my book tour with you made it so special. Thanks for the tremendous job of coordination and always listening. Also, thanks to all the people that worked behind the scenes on my cookbook, from design to distribution. To Baton Rouge, for such fabulous hometown support. And to all "my people" who continue to use my cookbooks and make "trim and terrific" an everyday term in their homes. Thank you!

Contents

Contents

Introduction

"I don't have time to prepare dinner, and even if I did, I don't know what to make!" I hear these familiar words over and over. With this in mind, I am very excited to present my new collection of recipes, *Trim & Terrific One-Dish Favorites*.

These days everyone has a busy schedule and our hectic lifestyles don't leave much time to spend in the kitchen. Yet, our favorite pastime is still eating. With these one-dish meals, it is easy to get a complete, balanced meal on the table without all the fuss. More important, all of the recipes are very flavorful and will leave you feeling satisfied. Remember: I don't like diets or anything that tastes like cardboard. I love to eat good food and the criteria for all of the recipes is that they have to be delicious. You'll be surprised at how many people (including yourself!) will ask, "Is this really low fat?"

But is doesn't matter how delicious a dish is if you don't have the time or energy to cook it. One-dish meals have always had great appeal, and they seem to be enjoying renewed popularity. I am a working mother of three, and there never seems to be enough time in the day to get it all done. One-dish meals make your life easier in several ways: Most recipes can be prepared in advance, many require almost no attention while they cook, and most can be assembled quickly, providing a nutritionally complete dish. And the best part, there's very little clean-up! But don't think that a one-dish meal can't be fit for company: Many dishes in this book are guaranteed to impress even the most important guests.

Most of the ingredients called for in these recipes are probably already in your pantry or refrigerator! And I firmly believe in one-stop shopping—everything in this book is readily available at your local grocery store. Also, you will not find ingredients such as egg substitutes or fake butter flakes in my recipes, but you will find convenience products like canned soups, frozen vegetables, and cake mixes. Convenience products are exactly that…products designed to add convenience to your life!

Each recipe in this book gets 30 percent or less of its calories from fat, and the nutritional analysis has been calculated by Pennington Biomedical Research Center. For those who are sodium-conscious, I have used no-salt-added tomato products, and I call for salt and pepper to taste in the recipes. In the back of the book, diabetic exchanges are provided for those who need them. Throughout the book, there is a ♥ on the recipes that have a cholesterol count of 60 mg or less per serving. When an optional ingredient is included in the recipe, it is not calculated for in the nutritional analysis, and the analysis is based on the larger number of servings.

As you glance through *Trim & Terrific One-Dish Favorites,* you will find oven casseroles, main-course soups and salads, skillet dishes, even brunch dishes and desserts. For my vegetarian friends, I've included meatless main dishes, and of course I've kept the very popular pasta and Southwestern sections that have appeared in my earlier books. I hope you will enjoy these recipes. People continually let me know how much they like cooking from my books, and they are often pleased to report that the pounds have faded away. I believe there should be a balance in our lives, and that a low-fat diet, with some splurges here and there, can be part of a healthy, fulfilling lifestyle. My goal is to share the philosophy and recipes that work for me and my family, and to help all my readers become "Trim and Terrific."

Menus

Here are some suggested occasions for trying these one-dish favorites. If you wish, serve a simple side dish. I have included brunch and desserts in the lists, too.

Simply Sunday

Crustless Spinach and Mushroom Quiche (page 9)

Broccoli Soup (page 17)

Swiss Steak (page 80)

Southwestern Pot Roast (page 159)

Old-Fashioned Pork Chop Casserole (page 93)

Banana Pudding Surprise (page 194)

German Chocolate Cake (page 189)

Weekend Casually

Rice Taco Salad (page 146)

Paella Salad (page 54)

Roasted Eye of Round and Vegetables (page 89)

Italian Chicken (page 67)

Turkey and Rice Bake (page 78)

Children's Choice

Baked Waffles and Ham (page 10)

Sloppy Joes (page 83)

Hearty Hamburger Meal (page 84)

Meat Sauce with Angel Hair Pasta (page 133)

Macaroni and Cheese Soup (page 25)

Meatball Stew (page 33)

Simple Chicken Combo (page 66)

Chicken, Barley, and Bow-Tie Soup (page 23)

Company's Coming: Quick

Sirloin Strips with Dijon Mushroom Sauce (page 86)

Pork Tenderloin Diane (page 96)

Cheesy Shrimp-Rice Casserole (page 106)

Chocolate Trifle (page 196)

Formal Affair

Southwestern Shrimp and Black Bean Chili (page 36)

Crabmeat au Gratin (page 117)

Shrimp with Oranges and Pasta (page 124)

Salmon Fettuccine (page 130)

Penne with Spinach, Sun-Dried Tomatoes, and Goat Cheese (page 138)

Summer Sizzlers

Zucchini Frittata (page 11)

Spicy Corn and Squash Chowder (page 18)

Tex-Mex Chicken Chowder (page 24)

Garden Pasta (page 168)

Squash, Tomato, and Bow-Tie Pasta (page 168)

Italian Pork, Squash, and Tomatoes (page 97)

Blueberry Poppyseed Cake (page 190)

Great Grillers

Beef and Salsa Fajitas (page 149)

Chicken and Beef Shish Kabobs (page 81)

Chilled Soups

Gazpacho with Shrimp (page 14)

Vichyssoise (page 14)

Holiday Heroes

Orange-Glazed Cornish Hens with Rice Stuffing (page 75)

Glazed Turkey with Cornbread Stuffing (page 77)

Cranberry Chicken with Wild Rice (page 73)

Smoked Turkey and Wild Rice Salad (page 51)

Shower Salads

Chicken Salad Olé (page 144)

Vermicelli Feta Salad (page 44)

Waldorf Pasta Salad (page 43)

Shrimp and Rice Salad (page 52)

Tomatoes Stuffed with Wild Rice Salad (page 175)

Chicken Leftovers

Creamy Chicken and Spinach (page 63)

Chunky Chicken Divan (page 58)

Chicken and Potatoes Picante (page 60)

Chicken Pot Pie (page 62)

Mexican Chicken Casserole (page 154)

Southern Brunch

Tex-Mex Eggs (page 155)

Mexican Brunch Biscuit Bake (page 7)

Breakfast Tortillas Santa Fe (page 8)

Midday Brunch

Steak Creole with Cheese Grits (page 12)

Sweet Breakfast

Blueberry Pancakes (page 2)

Baked French Toast (page 3)

Tuna Testimonials

Tuna Artichoke Pasta Salad (page 42)

Tex-Mex Tuna Salad (page 146)

Tuna-Orzo Salad (page 41)

Tuna Macaroni Casserole (page 139)

Italian Ideas

Italian Scramble (page 4)

Pizza-Baked Fish (page 113)

Shrimp Ziti Primavera (page 127)

Manicotti (page 136)

Lasagne Lovers

Crispy Southwestern Lasagne (page 157)

Plentiful Pork Soup
(page 30)

Shrimp, White Bean, and Pasta
Soup (page 20)

Pork Chop and Lima Bean Skillet
Supper (page 94)

Meat Sauce with Angel Hair Pasta
(page 133)

Chili (page 34)

Enchilada Casserole
(page 158)

Chocolate Black Forest Upside-
Down Cake (page 188)

Dazzling Desserts

Chocolate Trifle (page 196)

Caramel Cheesecake (page 200)

Pick-Up Squares

Marbled Brownies (page 183)

Loaded Brownies (page 182)

Apricot Crumble Squares
(page 186)

Quick Cakes

Peach Almond Dump Cake
(page 188)

Quickie Italian Cream Cake
(page 187)

German Chocolate Cake
(page 189)

Easy Mocha Cake (page 192)

Summer Special Sweets

Peach and Blueberry Summer
Spectacular (page 198)

Nectarine Crumble (page 199)

Terrific Trifles

Chocolate Trifle (page 196)

Lemon Pineapple Trifle (page 197)

Casseroles for a Crowd

Tamale Pie (page 155)

Italian Meaty Pasta Dish
(page 134)

Italian Eggplant, Meat, and Rice
(page 82)

Chicken Florentine (page 64)

Paella Salad (page 54)

To Take to a Sick Friend

Chicken, Barley, and Bow-Tie
Soup (page 23)

Mexican Chicken Casserole
(page 154)

Chicken and Artichoke Vermicelli
(page 120)

Apricot Sponge Cake (page 185)

Quickie Italian Cream Cake
(page 187)

BRUNCH

Blueberry Pancakes ♥

These pancakes are so good you won't need much syrup or margarine.

1 cup low-fat buttermilk	1 teaspoon baking powder
4 large egg whites	½ teaspoon baking soda
2 tablespoons sugar	1 cup blueberries, fresh or
1½ tablespoons canola oil	frozen (thawed)
1 cup all-purpose flour	

In a large mixing bowl, beat together the buttermilk, egg whites, sugar, and oil. In a another mixing bowl, combine together the flour, baking powder, and baking soda. Add the flour mixture to the buttermilk mixture, blending well. Stir the blueberries in gently. Coat a nonstick skillet with nonstick cooking spray and heat over medium-high heat. Pour the batter in ¼-cup portions onto the pan and cook until brown on both sides and firm to touch, about 3 minutes per side.

Makes 10 to 12 pancakes

Nutritional information per serving

Calories	164	Cal. from Fat (%) 22.8		Sodium (g)	267
Fat (g)	4.2	Saturated Fat (g)	0.5	Cholesterol (mg)	1
Protein (g)	6	Carbohydrate (g) 25.7			

All-American Egg Bake

Potatoes, bacon, cheese, and chilies are quickly thrown together to create a very satisfying dish.

4 ounces Canadian bacon, chopped	1 (12-ounce) container fat-free cottage cheese
1½ pounds red potatoes, peeled and coarsely chopped	⅓ cup self-rising flour
4 large eggs	1½ cups shredded reduced-fat Cheddar cheese
5 large egg whites	1 (4-ounce) can diced green chilies, drained

Preheat the oven to 350° F. In a large skillet coated with nonstick cooking spray, cook the Canadian bacon over medium heat for 3 minutes. Add the potatoes and sauté, stirring, until tender and lightly browned, about 10 to 12 minutes. Whisk together the eggs and egg whites in a large mixing bowl. Add the Canadian bacon, cottage cheese, flour, potatoes, Cheddar, and green chilies and stir to blend. Transfer to a 3-quart oblong casserole coated with nonstick cooking spray. Bake for 30 to 35 minutes.

Makes 10 to 12 servings

Nutritional information per serving

Calories	162	Cal. from Fat (%) 30.1		Sodium (g)	449
Fat (g)	5.4	Saturated Fat (g)	2.8	Cholesterol (mg)	88
Protein (g)	14.4	Carbohydrate (g) 12.9			

Baked French Toast ♥

The orange juice and maple syrup make this a light, not-too-sweet breakfast.

3 tablespoons light stick
  margarine, melted
⅓ cup maple syrup
1 teaspoon ground cinnamon
1 large egg

4 large egg whites
1 cup orange juice
8 slices white or whole
  wheat bread

Preheat the oven to 375° F. Combine the margarine and syrup together in a $13 \times 9 \times 2$-inch baking pan and sprinkle with the cinnamon. In a mixing bowl, beat together the egg, egg whites, and orange juice. Dip the bread into the egg mixture and arrange in a single layer in the baking pan. Bake for 20 to 25 minutes, or until the bread is light brown.

Makes 8 servings

Nutritional information per serving

Calories	162	Cal. from Fat (%) 25.8		Sodium (g)	229
Fat (g)	4.6	Saturated Fat (g)	1	Cholesterol (mg)	27
Protein (g)	4.9	Carbohydrate (g)	4.6		

Italian Scramble

When you need to feed a group of people, this fabulous egg dish is so much easier than individual omelets. With the spices, ham, and cheeses, it's definitely a dish you must try.

1¼ cups sliced mushrooms
¼ pound ham, diced
1 teaspoon minced garlic
1 medium green bell
  pepper, seeded and
  chopped
3 large eggs
5 large egg whites
1 teaspoon dried basil

1 teaspoon dried oregano
Salt and pepper to taste
½ teaspoon crushed red
  pepper flakes
4 ounces fat-free cream
  cheese, softened
1 cup shredded part-skim
  mozzarella cheese
  (optional)

In a large skillet coated with nonstick cooking spray, cook the mushrooms, ham, garlic, and green pepper over medium heat, until tender, about 5 minutes. Remove with a slotted spoon and set aside. In a large mixing bowl, whisk together the eggs, egg whites, basil, oregano, salt and pepper, and red pepper flakes. Cut the cream cheese into small pieces and add to the egg mixture. In a large skillet coated with nonstick cooking spray, cook the egg mixture over medium heat, folding with a spatula to blend in the cream cheese. When the eggs are half set, add the vegetable mixture and the mozzarella, if desired. Continue to cook while gently folding in the cheese and vegetables with a spatula. When the eggs are done and the cheese is melted, serve immediately.

Makes 6 servings

Nutritional information per serving

Calories	98	Cal. from Fat (%)	30.7	Sodium (g)	410
Fat (g)	3.3	Saturated Fat (g)	0.8	Cholesterol (mg)	115
Protein (g)	12.6	Carbohydrate (g)	4		

Tex-Mex Eggs

The cumin helps give this filling breakfast dish its Southwestern flavor.

5 (6-inch) corn tortillas
1 bunch green onions (scallions), finely chopped
1 red bell pepper, seeded and chopped
2 tablespoons chopped jalapeño pepper
¼ cup finely chopped fresh cilantro

2 large eggs
6 large egg whites
¼ cup skim milk
1 teaspoon ground cumin
Salt and pepper to taste
⅓ cup shredded reduced-fat sharp Cheddar cheese

Preheat the oven to 500° F. Dip the tortillas into water, drain, and place on a baking sheet coated with nonstick cooking spray. Bake for 4 minutes, turn, and bake for 2 minutes longer, or until crisp. Set aside. In a large skillet coated with nonstick cooking spray, cook the green onions, red pepper, and jalapeño over medium-high heat, sautéing, until tender, about 4 minutes. Transfer to a mixing bowl and stir in the cilantro. In another mixing bowl, combine the eggs, egg whites, milk, cumin, and salt and pepper. Crumble the crisp tortillas into the egg mixture; let stand for 5 minutes. Pour the egg mixture into a skillet coated with nonstick cooking spray over medium heat. As the mixture begins to cook, gently lift the edges with a spatula and tilt the pan to allow the uncooked portions to flow underneath. When the eggs are almost set, spoon the vegetable mixture over the top, mixing. Sprinkle with Cheddar and continue cooking until the eggs are done and the cheese is melted.

Makes 4 servings

Nutritional information per serving

Calories	171	Cal. from Fat (%)	28.4	Sodium (g)	325
Fat (g)	5.4	Saturated Fat (g)	2.2	Cholesterol (mg)	113
Protein (g)	13.6	Carbohydrate (g)	17.4		

Western Breakfast Rice

When you've run out of fresh ideas for brunch, try this delicious rice hash-type dish full of vegetables.

1 cup chopped onion
1 green bell pepper, seeded and chopped
1 cup sliced mushrooms
¾ cup chopped tomato
2 large eggs, lightly beaten
5 large egg whites, lightly beaten

½ cup skim milk
Salt and pepper to taste
4 cups cooked brown rice
½ cup shredded reduced-fat Cheddar cheese

In a skillet coated with nonstick cooking spray, cook the onion, green pepper, mushrooms, and tomato over medium-high heat, until tender, about 5 minutes. In a mixing bowl, combine the eggs, egg whites, milk, and salt and pepper. Reduce the heat to medium and pour the egg mixture over the vegetables. Continue cooking, stirring, for 3 to 4 minutes. Add the rice and Cheddar, stirring, and cook for 2 minutes longer, or until the eggs are done and the cheese is melted. Serve immediately.

Makes 6 servings

Nutritional information per serving

Calories	243	Cal. from Fat (%)	18.5	Sodium (g)	163
Fat (g)	5	Saturated Fat (g)	2.1	Cholesterol (mg)	78
Protein (g)	11.9	Carbohydrate (g)	37		

Florentine English Muffins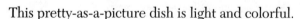

This pretty-as-a-picture dish is light and colorful.

2 (10-ounce) packages frozen chopped spinach
1 tablespoon all-purpose flour
1 cup skim milk
Dash of ground nutmeg

Salt and pepper to taste
5 English muffins, cut in half
10 slices tomato
1 cup shredded part-skim mozzarella cheese

Preheat the broiler. Cook the spinach according to package directions. Drain very well. In a saucepan, mix the flour and milk and cook over medium heat until thickened, about 5 minutes. Stir in the spinach, nutmeg, and salt and pepper. Lay the English muffin halves on a baking sheet. Divide the spinach mixture evenly on top of the muffins. Top each muffin with a tomato slice and sprinkle evenly with the mozzarella. Place under the broiler for 2 minutes, or until the cheese is melted and the muffin begins to brown. Watch carefully.

Makes 10 servings

Nutritional information per serving

Calories	127	Cal. from Fat (%)	19	Sodium (g)	244
Fat (g)	2.7	Saturated Fat (g)	1.4	Cholesterol (mg)	7
Protein (g)	7.8	Carbohydrate (g)	18.7		

Mexican Brunch Biscuit Bake

There is so little work needed to create this spicy, very tasty dish. And it's a great choice for those looking for an eggless morning treat.

2 (7½-ounce) cans of 10-
count buttermilk biscuits
1 (16-ounce) jar chunky salsa
1 bunch green onions
(scallions), chopped

1 cup shredded reduced-fat
Monterey Jack cheese

Preheat the oven to 350° F. Separate the biscuits and cut each into quarters. In a large mixing bowl, toss the biscuits with the salsa, green onions, and Monterey Jack. Transfer this mixture into a 13 × 9 × 2-inch baking dish coated with nonstick cooking spray. Bake, uncovered, for 30 minutes, or until the middle is fully cooked.

Makes 8 to 10 servings

Nutritional information per serving

Calories	160	Cal. from Fat (%)	24.5	Sodium (g)	943
Fat (g)	4.4	Saturated Fat (g)	2.1	Cholesterol (mg)	8
Protein (g)	5.9	Carbohydrate (g)	24.5		

Breakfast Tortillas Santa Fe

This is one of the most outstanding tortilla bake recipes. It's like breakfast enchiladas!

½ teaspoon minced garlic
½ cup chopped onion
¼ cup all-purpose flour
2¼ cups skim milk, divided
1 (4-ounce) can diced green chilies, drained
Salt and pepper to taste
½ cup chopped green bell pepper

3 large eggs
5 large egg whites
¼ cup sliced green onions (scallions)
8 (8-inch) flour tortillas
1 cup shredded reduced-fat Monterey Jack cheese

Preheat the oven to 350° F. In a medium pot coated with nonstick cooking spray, sauté the garlic and onion over medium-high heat until tender, about 3 minutes. Stir together the flour and 2 cups of the milk and add to the garlic and onion, stirring and cooking, until thickened, about 7 minutes. Add the green chilies and salt and pepper. Remove from the heat and set aside. In a medium skillet coated with nonstick cooking spray, sauté the green pepper over medium heat until tender, about 3 minutes. In a mixing bowl, whisk together the eggs, egg whites, and the remaining milk. Pour over the green pepper and cook, stirring, until the eggs are almost done, about 3 to 5 minutes. Stir in the green onions and cook until the eggs are done. Divide the egg mixture (about ¼ cup per tortilla) evenly down the middle of each tortilla. Spoon a heaping tablespoon of the chili sauce on each tortilla. Roll up and place, seam side down, in a 13 × 9 × 2-inch pan coated with nonstick cooking spray. Spoon the remaining sauce over the tortillas and sprinkle with the Monterey Jack. Bake, uncovered, for 15 to 20 minutes, or until the tortillas are well heated and the cheese is melted.

Makes 8 tortillas

Nutritional information per serving

Calories	.	296	Cal. from Fat (%) 26.8		Sodium (g)	465
Fat (g)		8.8	Saturated Fat (g)	3.3	Cholesterol (mg)	91
Protein (g)		15.7	Carbohydrate (g)	38.5		

Crustless Spinach and Mushroom Quiche ♥

Quiche also makes a lovely lunch offering, especially if you include the sausage.

½ pound mushrooms, sliced
1 onion, chopped
1 teaspoon minced garlic
½ cup chopped low-fat
   smoked sausage (optional)
1 (10-ounce) package frozen
   chopped spinach, thawed
   and squeezed dry

2 large eggs
4 large egg whites
1 cup nonfat sour cream
1 tablespoon Dijon mustard
Salt and pepper to taste
1 cup shredded part-skim
   mozzarella cheese

Preheat the oven temperature to 350° F. In a skillet coated with nonstick cooking spray, sauté the mushrooms, onion, garlic, and sausage over medium-high heat until tender, about 5 minutes. Stir in the spinach. In a mixing bowl, combine together the egg, egg whites, sour cream, mustard, and salt and pepper. Mix in the spinach mixture and the mozzarella. Spoon the spinach mixture into the prepared pastry shell. Bake, uncovered, for 40 to 45 minutes, or until set.

Makes 6 to 8 servings

Nutritional information per serving

Calories	116	Cal. from Fat (%)	30.5	Sodium (g)	205
Fat (g)	3.9	Saturated Fat (g)	2	Cholesterol (mg)	6.6
Protein (g)	9.7	Carbohydrate (g)	9.6		

Baked Waffles and Ham

This is a very kid-friendly recipe, highlighting the popular flavor combo of waffles, ham, and syrup.

2 cups skim milk
2 large eggs
1 large egg white
⅓ cup maple syrup
1 teaspoon vanilla extract

1 (10-ounce) package frozen
  square waffles
6 ounces baked ham, diced
½ cup shredded reduced-fat
  Cheddar cheese

In a large bowl, whisk together the milk, eggs, egg white, syrup, and vanilla until blended. Arrange 4 of the waffles side by side in a 13 × 9 × 2-inch baking dish coated with nonstick cooking spray. Sprinkle evenly with the ham, then top with the remaining 4 waffles. Pour the milk mixture over all, cover with foil, and let stand for 30 minutes at room temperature. Preheat the oven to 350° F. Set the foil-covered baking pan on the top rack and bake for 20 minutes. Remove the foil, sprinkle the Cheddar on top, and bake 10 minutes more, or until the cheese is melted.

Makes 6 servings

Nutritional information per serving

Calories	301	Cal. from Fat (%) 29.6		Sodium (g)	887
Fat (g)	9.9	Saturated Fat (g) 3.4		Cholesterol (mg)	104
Protein (g)	15.8	Carbohydrate (g) 36.6			

Zucchini Frittata

A frittata is a sort of Italian omelet that has the filling ingredients blended into the eggs. This one features zucchini, tomatoes, and cheese.

1 cup chopped onion
1 teaspoon minced garlic
3 cups shredded zucchini
   (about 3 medium)
Salt and pepper to taste
3 large eggs
5 large egg whites
½ cup skim milk

1 teaspoon dried basil
3 tablespoons all-purpose
   flour
1 cup shredded reduced-fat
   mozzarella cheese
3 Roma (plum) tomatoes,
   sliced

Preheat the oven to 350° F. In a large skillet coated with nonstick cooking, sauté the onion and garlic over medium heat until tender, about 5 minutes. Add the zucchini to the onion and garlic and cook for 2 minutes. Season with salt and pepper. In a large bowl, beat the eggs, egg whites, and milk. Whisk the basil and flour into the eggs. Stir in the onion-zucchini mixture and the mozzarella. Pour the mixture into an 2-quart oblong baking dish coated with nonstick cooking spray. Arrange the tomato slices on top. Bake, uncovered, for 30 to 35 minutes, or until set. Let cool slightly before cutting.

Makes 8 servings

Nutritional information per serving

Calories	117	Cal. from Fat (%)	30.3	Sodium (g)	143
Fat (g)	3.9	Saturated Fat (g)	1.9	Cholesterol (mg)	85
Protein (g)	10.4	Carbohydrate (g)	9.9		

Steak Creole with Cheese Grits

This might be the best-tasting dish in this book. I never thought round steak could taste so good, and combined with the cheese grits it is hard to beat. This great brunch dish is a true Southern delight. You can also serve it as a light evening meal.

3 pounds lean, boneless top round steak	1 (15-ounce) can no-salt-added tomato sauce
¼ teaspoon pepper	1 teaspoon light brown sugar
¼ cup all-purpose flour	1 tablespoon Worcestershire
1 onion, thickly sliced	sauce
2 green bell pepper, seeded and sliced	1 teaspoon dried basil
	1 teaspoon dried thyme
1 tablespoon minced garlic	1 teaspoon dried oregano
2 cups canned beef broth	Cheese Grits (recipe follows)

Trim any fat from the round steak. Season the steak with the pepper and dredge in the flour, shaking off any excess. In a large skillet coated with nonstick cooking spray, brown the steak over medium-high heat for 5 to 7 minutes on each side. Remove the steak and set aside. Add the onion and pepper to the skillet and cook over moderate heat, stirring occasionally, about 5 minutes. Stir in the garlic, beef broth, tomato sauce, brown sugar, Worcestershire sauce, basil, thyme, and oregano and bring to a boil. Return the steak to the skillet and spoon some of the sauce over it. Cover and cook over medium-low heat for 1½ to 2 hours, or until the steak is very tender, stirring occasionally. Serve with the grits.

Makes 6 servings

Cheese Grits

1 cup quick grits	1 cup shredded reduced-fat
3 cups water	Cheddar cheese

Cook the grits according to package directions, using 3 cups water and omitting any salt. After they are done, stir in the Cheddar.

Nutritional information per serving

Calories	487	Cal. from Fat (%) 19.2		Sodium (g)	578
Fat (g)	10.4	Saturated Fat (g)	4.8	Cholesterol (mg)	143
Protein (g)	61.7	Carbohydrate (g) 32.9			

SOUPS, STEWS, AND CHILIS

Gazpacho with Shrimp

This terrific chilled tomato-based soup is full of veggies and shrimp. It's a great make-ahead dish.

6 cups tomato juice
2 tablespoons red wine
  vinegar
1 tablespoon minced garlic
1 cup finely chopped green
  bell pepper
½ cup finely chopped red
  bell pepper
1½ cups finely chopped
  tomato

½ cup chopped onion
1 cup chopped green onions
  (scallions)
1 teaspoon dried basil
1 teaspoon dried oregano
Dash of hot pepper sauce
½ teaspoon pepper
1 pound small cooked
  peeled shrimp

In a large bowl, mix together the tomato juice, vinegar, and garlic. In another bowl, combine the green pepper, red pepper, tomato, onion, and green onions. Add half the vegetable mixture to the tomato juice mixture. Place the remaining half of the vegetable mixture in a food processor and process until smooth. Add to the tomato juice mixture. Stir in the basil, oregano, hot sauce, pepper, and shrimp. Refrigerate, covered, until well chilled, or overnight.

Makes 8 servings

Nutritional information per serving

Calories	94	Cal. from Fat (%)	7.4	Sodium (g)	759
Fat (g)	0.8	Saturated Fat (g)	0.2	Cholesterol (mg)	81
Protein (g)	10.9	Carbohydrate (g)	13		

Vichyssoise ♥

Serve this enduring favorite in chilled bowls with chives or chopped green onions sprinkled on top. Vichyssoise is always a good standby, mild enough for children but sophisticated enough for grown-ups.

1 tablespoon light stick
  margarine
1 onion, chopped
3 baking potatoes, peeled
  and diced
2 (16-ounce) cans fat-free
  chicken broth

1 (12-ounce) can evaporated
  skimmed milk
1 cup skim milk
½ cup nonfat sour cream
Salt and pepper to taste

In a large pot coated with nonstick cooking spray, melt the margarine and sauté the onion until tender. Add the potatoes, chicken broth, and evaporated milk. Bring to a boil, lower the heat, and simmer until the potatoes are tender, about 15 minutes. Transfer to a food processor or blender and puree. Whisk in the skim milk and sour cream. Season with salt and pepper. Refrigerate, covered, and serve cold.

Makes 8 servings

Nutritional information per serving

Calories	140	Cal. from Fat (%)	7.9	Sodium (g)	372
Fat (g)	1.2	Saturated Fat (g)	0.3	Cholesterol (mg)	5
Protein (g)	7.4	Carbohydrate (g)	23.9		

Pasta Tomato Soup Florentine

Pasta and fresh spinach give this tomato-based soup pizzazz.

1 onion, chopped
1 (46-ounce) can 100%
   vegetable juice
1 (14½-ounce) can no-salt-
   added diced tomatoes,
   with their juices
1 (10-ounce) can diced
   tomatoes and green
   chilies, drained

2 (14½-ounce) cans
   vegetable broth
1 tablespoon dried oregano
1 teaspoon sugar
2 cups rotini pasta
1 bunch fresh spinach,
   washed and stemmed
6 tablespoons grated
   Parmesan cheese

In a large pot coated with nonstick cooking spray, sauté the onion for 5 minutes, or until tender. Add the vegetable juice, tomatoes, tomatoes and chilies, vegetable broth, oregano, and sugar. Bring to a boil. Add the pasta and continue cooking for 10 minutes. Add the spinach and cook for 5 minutes longer. Sprinkle each serving with 1 tablespoon Parmesan.

Makes 6 servings

Nutritional information per serving

Calories	265	Cal. from Fat (%)	9.5	Sodium (g)	18.42
Fat (g)	2.8	Saturated Fat (g)	1.7	Cholesterol (mg)	4
Protein (g)	10.8	Carbohydrate (g)	50.2		

Two-Potato Bisque

Here's a different twist on bisque. The cilantro is optional, but it gives this dish the finishing touch.

1 large sweet potato, peeled
   and cut into 1-inch cubes
1 large baking potato,
   peeled and cut into 1-inch
   cubes
1 large onion, chopped
2 garlic cloves, minced
1 bay leaf
Salt to taste

1 teaspoon dried thyme
⅛ teaspoon cayenne pepper
2 cups canned fat-free
   chicken broth
1 cup low-fat buttermilk
1 cup skim milk
2 tablespoons lime juice
3 tablespoons chopped fresh
   cilantro

In a large pot, combine the sweet potato, potato, onion, garlic, bay leaf, salt, thyme, cayenne, and chicken broth and bring to a boil. Reduce the heat and simmer, covered, for 15 minutes, or until the potatoes are tender. Pour the mixture into a food processor and blend until smooth; return to the pot. Add the buttermilk, skim milk, and lime juice and cook over a low heat just until heated through; do not allow it to come to a boil. Sprinkle the cilantro on the top of each serving.

Makes 4 to 6 servings

Nutritional information per serving

Calories	99	Cal. from Fat (%)	5.6	Sodium (g)	257
Fat (g)	0.6	Saturated Fat (g)	0.3	Cholesterol (mg)	2
Protein (g)	4.7	Carbohydrate (g)	18.9		

Broccoli Soup ♡

This recipe uses *fresh* broccoli florets, which cook just as quickly as frozen and give this popular soup a great flavor. The vegetable broth keeps my vegetarian friends happy, but chicken broth can be used.

4 cups fresh broccoli florets
1 onion, chopped
⅔ cup all-purpose flour
1½ cups skim milk
2 (14½-ounce) cans
    vegetable broth or fat-free
    chicken broth

1 cup shredded reduced-fat
    Monterey Jack cheese
Salt and pepper to taste
⅛ teaspoon dried thyme

Cook the broccoli in a microwave dish in ⅓ cup water, covered, for 8 to 10 minutes or until tender. Drain and set aside. In a large pot coated with nonstick cooking spray, sauté the onion over medium heat until softened, about 3 to 5 minutes. Combine the flour and milk and stir constantly until mixed. Stir into the onion. Gradually add the vegetable broth and the broccoli. Stir to combine. Turn the heat to medium-high and bring the mixture to a boil. Cook on medium-high heat for about 5 minutes. Transfer the soup to a food processor or blender, puree the soup, and return it to the pot over low heat. Add the Monterey Jack, salt and pepper, and thyme, and cook until heated through and the cheese is melted.

Makes 6 to 8 servings

Nutritional information per serving

Calories	152	Cal. from Fat (%)	29.6	Sodium (g)	652
Fat (g)	5	Saturated Fat (g)	3.6	Cholesterol (mg)	16
Protein (g)	10.1	Carbohydrate (g)	17.2		

Spicy Corn and Squash Chowder ♥

One day I bought some squash and mixed it up with all my favorite ingredients to make this fabulous chowder. Give it a try even if you're not a squash person; you might surprise yourself!

1 pound yellow squash, thinly sliced
1 cup water
Salt and pepper to taste
1 onion, finely chopped
½ cup chopped green bell pepper
½ teaspoon minced garlic
1 large tomato, chopped

1 (15-ounce) can cream-style corn
1 (4-ounce) can diced green chilies, drained
1 (12-ounce) can evaporated skimmed milk
2 slices reduced-fat American cheese, cut into 1-inch pieces

Cook the squash in the water, covered, over medium-high heat with salt and pepper until the squash is tender, about 5 to 7 minutes. Drain and set aside. In a pot coated with nonstick cooking spray, sauté the onion and green pepper over medium heat until tender, about 5 minutes. Add the garlic and tomato and sauté for 2 minutes. Stir in the corn, green chilies, squash, and evaporated milk. Bring to a boil, reduce the heat, and add the American cheese, stirring, until the cheese is melted. Break the squash up with a fork.

Makes 4 servings

Nutritional information per serving

Calories	232	Cal. from Fat (%) 10.5		Sodium (g)	597
Fat (g)	2.7	Saturated Fat (g)	1.3	Cholesterol (mg)	9
Protein (g)	13.7	Carbohydrate (g) 43.2			

Shrimp and Corn Soup

This creamy soup is so easy it practically makes itself. Shrimp, corn, and green onions are a popular Louisiana combo. This wonderful recipe is high on my list, and will be on yours.

1 (10-ounce) can diced tomatoes and green chilies
1 large onion, chopped
½ teaspoon minced garlic
½ cup all-purpose flour
4 cups water
2 pounds medium shrimp, peeled and coarsely chopped, or small peeled shrimp

1 (16-ounce) package frozen corn
1 (15-ounce) can cream-style corn
1 bunch green onions (scallions), sliced
¼ cup chopped parsley
Salt and pepper to taste

Puree the tomatoes and green chilies in the food processor. In a large pot coated with nonstick cooking spray, sauté the onion and garlic over medium heat until tender, about 5 minutes. Sprinkle with the flour and mix. Gradually add the pureed tomatoes and chilies and water, stirring to mix in with the flour. Add the shrimp, frozen corn, and cream-style corn. Bring the mixture to a boil, lower the heat, and continue cooking, stirring occasionally, for about 5 to 7 minutes, or until the shrimp turn pink. Add the green onions and parsley. Season with salt and pepper.

Makes 8 servings

Nutritional information per serving

Calories	213	Cal. from Fat (%)	5.7	Sodium (g)	498
Fat (g)	1.3	Saturated Fat (g)	0.3	Cholesterol (mg)	161
Protein (g)	21.6	Carbohydrate (g)	31.4		

Shrimp, White Bean, and Pasta Soup

Super soup! The small amount of Canadian bacon gives the soup a burst of flavor that enhances the shrimp, beans, and pasta. This soup freezes well and is great on a cold night. If the soup gets too thick after storing in the refrigerator or freezer, you can add more water or chicken broth.

$\frac{1}{4}$ cup chopped Canadian bacon
1 onion, chopped
1 green bell pepper, seeded and chopped
1 teaspoon minced garlic
$1\frac{1}{2}$ pounds medium shrimp, peeled
$8\frac{1}{2}$ cups water, divided

1 (8-ounce) can no-salt-added tomato sauce
2 ($15\frac{1}{2}$-ounce) cans Great Northern beans, drained and rinsed
$1\frac{1}{2}$ cups rotini pasta
Salt and pepper to taste
1 bunch green onions (scallions), chopped

In a large pot coated with nonstick cooking spray, cook the bacon over medium heat until lightly browned, about 3 minutes. Add the onion, green pepper, and garlic, and sauté until the vegetables are tender, about 5 minutes. Add the shrimp and $\frac{1}{2}$ cup water and cook about 5 minutes. Add the tomato sauce, beans, and remaining water. Bring to a boil and add the pasta, cooking until it is done, about 6 to 8 minutes. Add the salt and pepper and green onions; heat for 1 minute and serve.

Makes 8 servings

Nutritional information per serving

Calories	255	Cal. from Fat (%)	6.2	Sodium (g)	394
Fat (g)	1.8	Saturated Fat (g)	0.4	Cholesterol (mg)	123
Protein (g)	23.8	Carbohydrate (g)	36.1		

Three-Bean Soup ♥

This is a fabulous vegetarian soup, but you can add ham or sausage to the onions for extra flavor when sautéing. I know you can find those packaged soups in the stores, but it really is fun to create your own.

1 cup dried red kidney beans	8 cups water
1 cup dried Great Northern beans	2 (10-ounce) cans diced tomatoes and green chilies, drained
1 cup dried black beans	1 (15-ounce) can no-salt-added tomato sauce
1 cup chopped onion	1½ teaspoons dried oregano
1 green bell pepper, seeded and chopped	1 teaspoon dried thyme
1 tablespoon minced garlic	2 bay leaves
1½ cups diced peeled carrots	Salt and pepper to taste

Sort and rinse the red kidney, Great Northern, and black beans; place in a large pot and cover with water. Let soak overnight. Drain and rinse. In a large pot coated with nonstick cooking spray, sauté the onion, green pepper, garlic, and carrots over medium-high heat for 3 to 5 minutes, until tender. Add the beans, the water, the tomatoes and green chilies, tomato sauce, oregano, thyme, and bay leaves; bring to a boil. Cover, reduce the heat, and continue cooking for 2 hours, or until the beans are tender. Remove the bay leaf and discard. Season with salt and pepper.

Makes 10 servings

Nutritional information per serving

Calories	206	Cal. from Fat (%)	3.6	Sodium (g)	249
Fat (g)	0.8	Saturated Fat (g)	0.2	Cholesterol (mg)	0
Protein (g)	13.2	Carbohydrate (g)	38.6		

Chicken, Shrimp, and Sausage Gumbo

This gumbo has it all—lots of seasoning as well as chicken, shrimp, and sausage. The ingredient list is a long one, but the dish is too good to miss. Brown the flour ahead of time to cut down on the final preparation time. I don't include okra because my kids don't like it, but it can be added if you like.

1½ cups all-purpose flour, divided
1 cup chopped celery
1 cup chopped green bell pepper
1 cup chopped onion
2 tablespoons minced garlic
½ teaspoon pepper
¼ teaspoon cayenne pepper
2½ pounds skinless, boneless chicken breasts, cut into chunks
1 (16-ounce) package low-fat smoked sausage

6 cups water
1 (16-ounce) can fat-free chicken broth
1 teaspoon dried basil
1 teaspoon dried oregano
1 teaspoon dried thyme
1 tablespoon Worcestershire sauce
2 bay leaves
2 pounds medium shrimp, peeled
1 bunch green onions (scallions), chopped
6 cups cooked rice

Preheat the oven to 350°F. Place 1 cup of the flour on a baking sheet with a rim and bake for 35 to 45 minutes, stirring frequently, until it is dark brown but not burned. In a large pot coated with non-stick cooking spray, sauté the celery, green pepper, onion, and garlic over medium heat until tender, about 8 minutes. Meanwhile, mix the remaining flour with the pepper and cayenne pepper. Coat the chicken with the flour mixture and add to the same pot, cooking until the chicken is brown, about 5 to 10 minutes. Meanwhile, cook the sausage in a pot of boiling water for 5 minutes to remove any excess grease. Drain, slice, and set aside. To the browned chicken, add the water, chicken broth, basil, oregano, thyme, Worcestershire sauce, and bay leaves. Bring to a boil and cook for 15 minutes, or until the chicken is tender. Lower the heat, add the shrimp and reserved sausage; continue cooking until the shrimp are done, about 7 to 10 minutes. Remove the bay leaves and discard. Add the green onions, heat for 1 minute, and serve over the rice in bowls.

Makes 8 servings

Calories	588	Cal. from Fat (%)	9.9	Sodium (g)	840
Fat (g)	6.5	Saturated Fat (g)	1.8	Cholesterol (mg)	271
Protein (g)	65.2	Carbohydrate (g)	62.7		

Chicken, Barley, and Bow-Tie Soup ♥

My kids always love chicken soup, and this hearty version with barley and pasta quickly became a favorite in my house.

2½ pounds skinless, boneless
   chicken breasts, cut into
   1-inch pieces
1 cup chopped celery
1½ cups chopped onion
2 cups thinly sliced peeled
   carrots
1 bay leaf

12 cups water
½ cup pearl barley
Salt and pepper to taste
½ teaspoon dried basil
3 chicken bouillon cubes
1 (16-ounce) package
   bow-tie pasta

Place the chicken, celery, onion, carrots, and bay leaf in a large pot filled with the water. Bring the water to a boil and add the barley. Reduce the heat, cover, and cook until the chicken and barley are done, about 30 minutes. Season with salt and pepper, and add the basil and bouillon cubes. Meanwhile, cook the pasta according to package directions, omitting oil and salt. Drain and set aside. Remove the bay leaf and add the pasta. Serve in bowls.

Makes 10 to 12 servings

Calories	315	Cal. from Fat (%)	9.5	Sodium (g)	350
Fat (g)	3.3	Saturated Fat (g)	0.8	Cholesterol (mg)	56
Protein (g)	27.5	Carbohydrate (g)	42.4		

Tex-Mex Chicken Chowder

This chunky chowder with a Southwestern personality is great served with tortilla chips.

1 tablespoon canola oil
1 teaspoon minced garlic
2 pounds skinless, boneless
  chicken breasts, cut into
  chunks
1 small onion, sliced
½ cup chopped green bell
  pepper
1 (14½-ounce) can fat-free
  chicken broth

1 (10-ounce) package frozen
  corn
1 (14½-ounce) can no-salt-
  added diced tomatoes,
  with their juices
3 yellow squash, thinly sliced
1 teaspoon ground cumin
Salt and pepper to taste
1 tablespoon chopped fresh
  cilantro

In a large pot, heat the oil over medium heat. Add the garlic and chicken, stirring to brown lightly on all sides, about 3 minutes. Add the onion and green pepper, and cook for 5 minutes, stirring. Add the chicken broth, bring to a boil, and simmer about 10 minutes. Add the corn, tomatoes, squash, cumin, and salt and pepper. Cover and cook over low heat 10 minutes, or until the squash is tender. Add the cilantro and cook for 2 minutes longer.

Makes 6 servings

Nutritional information per serving

Calories	291	Cal. from Fat (%)	20.1	Sodium (g)	243
Fat (g)	6.5	Saturated Fat (g)	1.3	Cholesterol (mg)	88
Protein (g)	37.7	Carbohydrate (g)	21.5		

Macaroni and Cheese Soup

When you say macaroni and cheese, you have the family's attention. This mild, creamy soup takes an old standby and adapts it into a great family meal, especially for the kids.

1 cup elbow pasta	½ teaspoon ground white
½ cup finely chopped peeled	pepper
carrots	2 tablespoons cornstarch
½ cup finely chopped onion	2 tablespoons water
4 cups skim milk	1 (10-ounce) package frozen
6 ounces reduced-fat	corn, thawed
pasteurized processed	½ cup frozen green beans,
cheese spread	thawed

Cook the pasta according to package directions, omitting any oil and salt. Drain, rinse with cold water, and set aside. In a large skillet coated with nonstick cooking spray, cook the carrots and onion over medium-high heat, stirring constantly, until tender, about 5 to 7 minutes. Add the milk and heat over low heat. Add the cheese and white pepper and stir until the cheese is melted. Combine the cornstarch and water, mixing well, and stir into the milk mixture. Cook over medium heat, stirring constantly, about 8 minutes, until the mixture thickens. Stir in the pasta, corn, and green beans, stirring constantly, until the beans are tender, about 5 minutes.

Makes 6 servings

Nutritional information per serving

Calories	254	Cal. from Fat (%) 14.4		Sodium (g)	511
Fat (g)	4	Saturated Fat (g) 2.3		Cholesterol (mg)	13
Protein (g)	15.9	Carbohydrate (g) 41			

Tortilla Soup ♥

It seems I always must include a tortilla soup recipe in each of my books. This is a simple way to make an excellent meal with a Southwestern touch out of leftover chicken.

1 cup chopped red onion	1 cup frozen corn, thawed
½ cup chopped red bell pepper	¼ cup chopped fresh cilantro
1 teaspoon minced garlic	¼ cup lime juice
1 (4-ounce) can chopped green chilies, drained	1 teaspoon ground cumin
8 cups canned fat-free chicken broth	1 cup broken tortilla chips
2 cups chopped cooked chicken breasts	½ cup to 1 cup shredded reduced-fat Monterey Jack cheese

In a large, heavy pot coated with nonstick cooking spray, sauté the onion, red pepper, and garlic over medium heat until tender, about 7 minutes. Add the chilies, chicken broth, chicken, corn, cilantro, lime juice, and cumin. Simmer, uncovered, for 10 minutes. Spoon into bowls and top with the broken tortilla chips and Monterey Jack.

Makes 4 to 6 servings

Nutritional information per serving

Calories	233	Cal. from Fat (%)	28.4	Sodium (g)	1,131
Fat (g)	7.3	Saturated Fat (g)	3	Cholesterol (mg)	50
Protein (g)	22.7	Carbohydrate (g)	19.2		

Veal, Mushroom, and Barley Soup ♥

A rich, thick soup for those cold days. The dill makes this soup delightfully different.

1 pound lean stewing veal, trimmed and cut into 2-inch chunks	2 cups sliced mushrooms
	8 cups canned fat-free chicken broth, plus more as needed
1 large onion, finely chopped	¾ cup pearl barley
½ cup finely chopped peeled carrots	1 teaspoon minced garlic
	1 teaspoon dried dillweed
⅓ cup finely chopped celery	Salt and pepper to taste

Coat a large pot with nonstick cooking spray and brown the veal on all sides over medium heat, about 8 minutes. Remove the veal and set aside. Add the onion, carrots, celery, and mushrooms and sauté until tender, about 5 to 7 minutes. Add the chicken broth, veal, and barley to the pot and bring to a boil. Cover loosely, reduce the heat, and simmer 45 minutes. Add the garlic, dillweed, and salt and pepper and continue simmering until the barley is tender, about 10 to 15 minutes. If the soup gets too thick, add more chicken broth.

Makes 6 servings

Nutritional information per serving

Calories	242	Cal. from Fat (%)	17	Sodium (g)	795
Fat (g)	4.6	Saturated Fat (g)	1.6	Cholesterol (mg)	40
Protein (g)	16.5	Carbohydrate (g)	33.2		

Southwestern Vegetable Soup

This tomato-based soup is an easy vegetarian Southwest favorite.

1 cup chopped onion
1 teaspoon minced garlic
2 cups sliced peeled carrots
1 pound red potatoes, peeled and cut into small chunks
2 (14½-ounce) cans vegetable broth
1 (15-ounce) can no-salt-added tomato sauce

1½ cups mild salsa
2 teaspoons dried oregano
2 teaspoons ground cumin
1 (10-ounce) package frozen corn
½ cup sliced green onions (scallions)
½ cup shredded reduced-fat Monterey Jack cheese

In a large pot coated with nonstick cooking spray, sauté the onion and garlic until tender over medium heat, about 3 to 5 minutes. Add the carrots, potatoes, vegetable broth, tomato sauce, salsa, oregano, cumin, and corn. Bring the mixture to a boil, lower the heat, and simmer for 20 minutes, or until the carrots and potatoes are tender. When serving, sprinkle each bowl with the green onions and Monterey Jack.

Makes 6 servings

Nutritional information per serving

Calories	216	Cal. from Fat (%)	12.2	Sodium (g)	1,552
Fat (g)	2.9	Saturated Fat (g)	2	Cholesterol (mg)	7
Protein (g)	7.2	Carbohydrate (g)	41.7		

Old-Fashioned Beefy Vegetable Stew

This traditional stew makes a rich, dark gravy that is wonderful served over the rice.

2 pounds sirloin tips, cut into
   2-inch chunks
1 onion, sliced
Salt and pepper to taste
2 (10½-ounce) cans beef
   consommé
¾ cup red wine

½ cup all-purpose flour
½ cup dry bread crumbs
1 (16-ounce) bag baby
   carrots
1 (10-ounce) package frozen
   peas
4 cups cooked rice

Preheat the oven to 350° F. Place the meat, onion, salt and pepper, consommé, and wine in a large, heavy pot. Combine the flour and bread crumbs in a bowl and stir into the meat mixture thoroughly. Cover and bake for 30 minutes. Reduce the heat to 300° F and cook 1½ hours longer, or until the meat is tender. Add the carrots and peas during the last 30 minutes of baking. Serve over the cooked rice.

Makes 6 to 8 servings

Nutritional information per serving

Calories	409	Cal. from Fat (%)	19.2	Sodium (g)	557
Fat (g)	8.7	Saturated Fat (g)	3.2	Cholesterol (mg)	68
Protein (g)	32	Carbohydrate (g)	45.2		

Tarragon Beef Stew

In the last half hour, you can add chunks of potatoes and sliced carrots and serve the stew in a bowl instead of over rice.

⅔ cup all-purpose flour
Salt and pepper to taste
1 tablespoon dried tarragon
½ teaspoon garlic powder
3 pounds sirloin tips, cut into
   1½-inch cubes
½ cup tarragon wine vinegar
1 cup canned beef broth

1 teaspoon sugar
1 (8-ounce) can whole
   mushrooms, with their
   juices
¼ cup chopped green onions
   (scallions)
6 cups cooked rice

Blend the flour with the salt and pepper, tarragon, and garlic powder in a shallow bowl. Coat the meat in the seasoned flour. Brown the meat in a large pot coated with nonstick cooking spray over medium heat, about 8 minutes. Stir in the vinegar, beef broth, and sugar and lower the heat. Cover and simmer 2 hours, or until the meat is tender. Add the mushrooms with their juices and the green onions. Cook, uncovered, for 10 minutes. Serve over the cooked rice.

Makes 8 servings

Nutritional information per serving

Calories	451	Cal. from Fat (%)	24	Sodium (g)	244
Fat (g)	12	Saturated Fat (g)	4.7	Cholesterol (mg)	102
Protein (g)	38.7	Carbohydrate (g)	44.2		

Veal Stew

This mild-flavored stew includes lots of veggies for flavor and color. If veal stew meat is not available, you can use another cut of veal and cut it into chunks. Veal is expensive, but the stew meat is usually more reasonable.

1½ pounds veal stew meat, or veal meat cut into 1½-inch cubes
Salt and pepper to taste
¼ cup all-purpose flour
1 (14½-ounce) can beef broth
2 tablespoons plum or currant jelly

1 cup pearl onions, peeled (frozen can be used)
2 cups baby carrots
½ pound mushrooms, halved
4 cups cooked rice or orzo pasta

Season the veal with the salt and pepper. In a large pot coated with nonstick cooking spray, cook the veal over medium-high heat until browned on all sides, about 5 to 7 minutes. Stir in the flour, mixing to coat. Gradually stir in the beef broth and jelly, mixing well. Bring the mixture to a boil, lower the heat, cover, and simmer for 20 minutes. Add the onions, carrots, and mushrooms and continue cooking, covered, about 40 minutes, or until the meat is tender, stirring occasionally. Serve over the rice or orzo.

Makes 4 to 6 servings

Nutritional information per serving

Calories	448	Cal. from Fat (%)	19.1	Sodium (g)	302
Fat (g)	9.5	Saturated Fat (g)	3.5	Cholesterol (mg)	85
Protein (g)	29.4	Carbohydrate (g)	59.1		

Plentiful Pork Soup

This delicious, hearty soup has a little of everything in it and lives up to its name.

1½ pounds pork tenderloin, cut into 2-inch chunks
1½ cups chopped onion
1 teaspoon minced garlic
1 teaspoon ground cumin
1 (6-ounce) package long-grain and wild rice
1 (15-ounce) can garbanzo beans, drained and rinsed
1 (16-ounce) can white beans (such as navy), drained and rinsed

2 (4-ounce) cans diced green chilies, drained
1 (11-ounce) can white shoe peg corn, drained
2 cups canned fat-free chicken broth
2 cups water
Salt and pepper to taste
1 cup shredded reduced-fat Monterey Jack cheese (optional)

In a large pot coated with nonstick cooking spray, add the pork, onion, and garlic and sauté for 8 to 10 minutes over medium heat, or until the pork browns and the onions are tender. Stir in the cumin, rice, garbanzo beans, white beans, green chilies, corn, chicken broth, and water. Bring to a boil, reduce the heat, cover, and simmer 40 to 45 minutes, or until the rice is done and the pork is tender. Season with salt and pepper. Serve in individual bowls and sprinkle with Monterey Jack, if desired.

Makes 10 to 12 servings

Nutritional information per serving

Calories	251	Cal. from Fat (%)	17.5	Sodium (g)	447
Fat (g)	4.9	Saturated Fat (g)	1.5	Cholesterol (mg)	43
Protein (g)	20.9	Carbohydrate (g)	31.6		

Different Twist Pork Stew

This new angle on stew would be great served with corn bread.

2 pounds pork tenderloin,
  trimmed of fat and cut into
  1½-inch cubes
1 large onion, chopped
1 (28-ounce) can no-salt-added
  tomatoes, with their juices
1 (14½-ounce) can fat-free
  chicken broth

2 bay leaves
Salt and pepper to taste
2 pounds sweet potatoes
  (about 4), peeled and cut
  into 1-inch cubes
1 (16-ounce) package frozen
  corn

In a large pot coated with nonstick cooking spray, brown the pork over low heat, about 5 minutes. Add the onion and cook until softened, about 7 minutes. Add the tomatoes, chicken broth, bay leaves, and salt and pepper. Cook for 30 minutes. Add the sweet potatoes and corn. Simmer until the sweet potatoes and pork are tender, about 45 minutes to 1 hour. Remove the bay leaves and discard before serving.

Makes 6 servings

Nutritional information per serving

Calories	439	Cal. from Fat (%)	16.2	Sodium (g)	252
Fat (g)	7.9	Saturated Fat (g)	2.6	Cholesterol (mg)	90
Protein (g)	37.9	Carbohydrate (g)	55		

Southwestern Pork Stew

Throw all these ingredients together in one pot for a super Southwestern stew.

2 teaspoons ground cumin
1 teaspoon chili powder
⅛ teaspoon cayenne pepper
1½ pounds pork tenderloin,
  trimmed of fat and cut into
  ¾-inch cubes
2 cups chopped onion
1 cup chopped green bell
  pepper
1 teaspoon minced garlic
4 cups cubed peeled baking
  potatoes (about 2 large)

2 cups no-salt-added
  vegetable juice cocktail
1 (14½-ounce) can no-salt-
  added diced tomatoes,
  with their juices
1 (11-ounce) can Mexicorn,
  drained
Chopped fresh cilantro
  (optional)

Combine the cumin, chili powder, and cayenne in a large heavy-duty zip-top plastic bag. Add the pork, seal the bag, and shake to coat the pork with the seasoning. Coat a large pot with nonstick cooking spray and heat over medium-high heat. Add the pork, onion, green pepper, and garlic; sauté 10 minutes until the vegetables are tender. Stir in the potatoes, vegetable juice cocktail, tomatoes, and corn. Bring to a boil, reduce the heat, and cover. Simmer about 40 to 50 minutes, or until the pork is tender. Sprinkle with cilantro, if desired.

Makes 6 servings

Nutritional information per serving

Calories	293	Cal. from Fat (%)	17.9	Sodium (g)	288
Fat (g)	5.8	Saturated Fat (g)	1.9	Cholesterol (mg)	67
Protein (g)	27.8	Carbohydrate (g)	32.5		

Meatball Stew

These tasty meatballs in a tomato gravy with rice and peas provide a hearty meal the whole family will enjoy.

2 pounds ground sirloin
2 large egg whites, lightly
  beaten
⅓ cup dry bread crumbs
1 tablespoon minced garlic
Salt and pepper to taste
1 teaspoon dried basil
1 teaspoon dried thyme
1 onion, finely chopped
1 green bell pepper, seeded
  and cut into ¼-inch
  squares

2 (14½-ounce) cans no-salt-
  added whole tomatoes,
  crushed, with their juices
1 (10¾-ounce) can no-salt-
  added tomato puree
1 (10½-ounce) can beef
  broth
⅔ cup long-grain rice
1 (10-ounce) package frozen
  green peas

Preheat the broiler. In a bowl, combine the meat, egg whites, bread crumbs, garlic, salt and pepper, basil, and thyme. Shape into 30 balls about 1½ inches in diameter. Place the meatballs on a baking sheet coated with nonstick cooking spray. Broil in the oven for 4 to 5 minutes, turn the meatballs, and continue broiling for 4 minutes longer, or until done. Remove from the broiler and set aside. In a large pot coated with nonstick cooking spray, sauté the onion and green pepper over medium heat until tender, about 5 minutes. Add the tomatoes, tomato puree, and beef broth. Bring to a boil and add the meatballs. Mix in the rice, cover, reduce the heat, and continue cooking for 20 minutes, or until the rice is done. Stir in the peas, cover, and continue cooking for 10 minutes, or until the peas are tender.

Makes 6 servings

Nutritional information per serving

Calories	401	Cal. from Fat (%)	19.2	Sodium (g)	356
Fat (g)	8.6	Saturated Fat (g)	3.3	Cholesterol (mg)	90
Protein (g)	38.9	Carbohydrate (g)	40.5		

Chili

Chili is great to have on hand in the freezer, so make extra and freeze it in containers. If you want the deluxe version, serve it with nonfat sour cream, green onions, Cheddar cheese, and even baked tortilla chips on the side. I always include a chili recipe in my books, and each one is a must to try!

2 pounds ground sirloin
1 large green bell pepper, seeded and coarsely chopped
1 large red bell pepper, seeded and coarsely chopped
1 large onion, coarsely chopped
1 teaspoon minced garlic
1 (28-ounce) can no-salt-added whole tomatoes, coarsely chopped, with their juices

1 (6-ounce) can no-salt-added tomato paste
1 cup canned beef broth, plus more as needed
1 (16-ounce) red kidney beans, drained and rinsed
1 (10-ounce) package frozen corn, thawed and drained
2 tablespoons chili powder
½ teaspoon ground cumin
Salt and pepper to taste

In a large pot coated with nonstick cooking spray, cook the meat, green and red peppers, onion, and garlic until the meat is done and the vegetables are tender, about 10 minutes. Add the tomatoes, tomato paste, beef broth, beans, corn, chili powder, cumin, and salt and pepper. Reduce the heat to low, cover, and simmer for 30 minutes. If the chili gets too thick, add more broth or water.

Makes 8 servings

Nutritional information per serving

Calories	287	Cal. from Fat (%)	21	Sodium (g)	283
Fat (g)	6.7	Saturated Fat (g)	2.4	Cholesterol (mg)	68
Protein (g)	29.8	Carbohydrate (g)	28.8		

White Chicken Chili ♡

If you forget to soak beans overnight, this is a great way to enjoy a fresh bean dish the same day: the quick-soak method.

1 pound dried Great
  Northern beans
1 large onion, chopped
1 teaspoon minced garlic
1 tablespoon chopped
  jalapeño pepper
1 tablespoon dried oregano
Dash of cayenne pepper
2 teaspoons ground cumin
Pinch of ground cloves
5 cups canned fat-free
  chicken broth

1 (10-ounce) can diced
  tomatoes and green
  chilies, drained
⅛ cup lime juice
3 cups chopped cooked
  boneless, skinless chicken
  breasts
½ cup chopped fresh
  cilantro (optional)
⅓ cup grated Parmesan
  cheese (optional)

Place the dried beans in a large pot and cover with water. Bring to a boil and boil for 1 minute. Remove from the heat, cover, and let stand for one hour. After one hour, add the onion, garlic, jalapeño, oregano, cayenne, cumin, cloves, and chicken broth. Bring to a boil. Reduce the heat and simmer, covered, for 1½ hours. Add the tomatoes and chilies, lime juice, and chicken. Continue cooking, covered, over low heat for 30 minutes, or until the beans are tender. Serve with chopped cilantro and Parmesan, if desired.

Makes 8 servings

Nutritional information per serving

Calories	284	Cal. from Fat (%)	8.7	Sodium (g)	536
Fat (g)	2.8	Saturated Fat (g)	0.8	Cholesterol (mg)	45
Protein (g)	30	Carbohydrate (g)	35.1		

Southwestern Shrimp and Black Bean Chili

A fabulous blend of flavors that produce an easily made dish. This dish includes my favorites: black beans, corn, and shrimp. Serve in bowls and you have a hearty dinner.

1 green bell pepper, seeded and chopped
1 red bell pepper, seeded and chopped
1 large onion, chopped
1 cup shredded peeled carrots
1 tablespoon finely chopped jalapeño pepper
½ teaspoon minced garlic
1 tablespoon chili powder

1½ teaspoons dried cumin
1 (16-ounce) can no-salt-added whole tomatoes, chopped, with their juices
1 (16-ounce) can black beans, drained and rinsed
½ cup water
1 pound medium shrimp, peeled
1 (10-ounce) package frozen corn

In a large pot coated with nonstick cooking spray, sauté the green and red peppers, onion, carrots, jalapeños, and garlic until tender, about 6 to 8 minutes. Stir in the chili powder, cumin, tomatoes, black beans, water, and shrimp and bring to a boil. Reduce the heat and cook for 3 to 5 minutes, or until the shrimp are pink. Add the corn and continue cooking 5 minutes longer.

Makes 4 to 6 servings

Nutritional information per serving

Calories	2,085	Cal. from Fat (%)	6	Sodium (g)	275
Fat (g)	1.4	Saturated Fat (g)	0.3	Cholesterol (mg)	108
Protein (g)	19.1	Carbohydrate (g)	31.3		

MAIN-DISH
SALADS

Spinach Chef Salad with Creamy Dressing ♡

With this creamy seasoned dressing, you won't even miss the cheese. Browning the ham gives the salad a richer flavor.

½ cup plain nonfat yogurt
½ cup nonfat sour cream
3 tablespoons skim milk
2 teaspoons dried basil
⅓ cup finely chopped green onions (scallions), green part only
1 teaspoon minced garlic
8 ounces thinly sliced ham, cut into ½-inch strips

1 (12-ounce) package spinach, washed, stemmed, and torn into pieces
½ pound mushrooms, sliced
1 cup chopped tomato
⅓ cup chopped green onions (scallions), white part only
1 cup croutons (optional)

In a bowl, combine together the yogurt, sour cream, milk, basil, green onions (green part only), and garlic. Cover and refrigerate for 30 to 45 minutes. In a skillet coated with nonstick cooking spray, sauté the ham over medium-high heat until lightly browned, about 3 minutes. Remove from the pan and let it cool. In a large bowl, combine the spinach, mushrooms, tomato, green onions (white part), and ham. Serve with the dressing and with the croutons, if desired.

Makes 6 servings

Nutritional information per serving

Calories	116	Cal. from Fat (%)	18.7	Sodium (g)	636
Fat (g)	2.4	Saturated Fat (g)	0.7	Cholesterol (mg)	22
Protein (g)	12.3	Carbohydrate (g)	11.9		

Crowd-Pleaser Pasta Salad

When you are asked to bring a dish to feed a group, this salad is the answer. It's chockful of great ingredients, and if you feel like it, you can substitute cubed cooked chicken for the shrimp.

1 pound fettuccine pasta	½ cup chopped red bell
1 (10-ounce) package frozen	pepper
green peas, thawed	¼ cup chopped parsley
1 cup sliced green onions	⅓ cup finely chopped red
(scallions)	onion
2 cups halved cherry	3 cups peeled cooked
tomatoes	medium shrimp
2 (14-ounce) cans quartered	Dill Dressing (recipe
artichoke hearts, drained	follows)

Cook the pasta according to package directions, omitting any oil and salt. Drain and let cool. In a large bowl, combine the pasta with the peas, green onions, tomatoes, artichoke hearts, red pepper, parsley, onion, and shrimp. Toss with the Dill Dressing and serve.

Makes 12 servings

Dill Dressing

1 pint plain nonfat yogurt	1 tablespoon prepared
¼ cup white wine vinegar	horseradish
2 teaspoons dried dillweed	

Combine the yogurt, vinegar, dillweed, and horseradish in a small bowl, mixing well.

Nutritional information per serving

Calories	248	Cal. from Fat (%) 5.1		Sodium (g)	277
Fat (g)	1.4	Saturated Fat (g) 0.3		Cholesterol (mg)	71
Protein (g)	17.6	Carbohydrate (g) 41.7			

Deli Pasta Salad

When you don't know what to prepare and have deli in the fridge, try this recipe for a quick, refreshing salad. Use the deli meat of your choice.

1 (12-ounce) package ziti or
    penne (tubular) pasta
½ cup low-fat ricotta cheese
2 tablespoons Dijon mustard
2 tablespoons balsamic
    vinegar
1 teaspoon sugar
¼ teaspoon pepper

1 (10-ounce) package frozen
    peas, thawed
1 cup diced baked ham,
    chicken, or turkey
⅓ cup chopped green onions
    (scallions)
½ cup chopped Roma (plum)
    tomatoes

Cook the pasta according to package directions, omitting any oil and salt. Drain and set aside. Meanwhile, mix the ricotta, mustard, vinegar, sugar, and pepper in a food processor or a blender until smooth, about 30 seconds. In a large bowl, combine the pasta, peas, ham, green onions, and tomatoes. Add the ricotta mixture and toss. Serve at once, or refrigerate.

Makes 4 to 6 servings

Nutritional information per serving

Calories	319	Cal. from Fat (%)	9.4	Sodium (g)	423
Fat (g)	3.3	Saturated Fat (g)	1.1	Cholesterol (mg)	19
Protein (g)	18.2	Carbohydrate (g)	54		

Curried Orzo Salad

This Caribbean delight will quickly be on your list if you enjoy curry. It would be great to serve with a cup of soup or include in a salad medley.

1 (16-ounce) package orzo
    pasta
1½ cups chopped celery
1 cup dark seedless raisins
1 (8-ounce) can sliced water
    chestnuts, drained
½ cup fat-free Italian
    dressing

⅓ cup finely chopped onion
¾ cup plain nonfat yogurt
1 tablespoon balsamic
    vinegar
1 teaspoon curry powder
½ teaspoon ground ginger
2 tablespoons honey
Salt to taste

Cook the pasta according to package directions, omitting any oil and salt. In a large bowl, combine the pasta, celery, raisins, and water chestnuts; mix well and set aside. In another bowl, combine the Italian dressing, onion, yogurt, vinegar, curry powder, ginger, honey, and salt, stirring well. Pour the dressing mixture over the pasta mixture and toss well. Cover and refrigerate until ready to serve.

Makes 8 servings

Nutritional information per serving

Calories	716	Cal. from Fat (%)	3.9	Sodium (g)	196
Fat (g)	3.1	Saturated Fat (g)	0.1	Cholesterol (mg)	0
Protein (g)	28.1	Carbohydrate (g)	142.1		

Tuna-Orzo Salad

I never thought tuna salad could be so good. The feta and seasonings lends a Greek touch and makes this dish a true hit. The tuna can be omitted for a simple Greek orzo salad.

1 cup orzo pasta	1 (6½-ounce) can chunk
2 cups chopped Roma	light tuna, packed in
(plum) tomatoes	spring water, drained
½ cup (2 ounces) crumbled	½ cup red wine vinegar
feta cheese	1 tablespoon olive oil
⅓ cup chopped red onion	½ teaspoon dried basil
2 tablespoons sliced ripe	½ teaspoon dried oregano
black olives	1 teaspoon minced garlic

Cook the pasta according to package directions, omitting any oil and salt. Drain and rinse. In a large bowl, combine the pasta with the tomatoes, feta, onion, olives, and tuna, tossing well. In a small bowl, combine the vinegar, oil, basil, oregano, and garlic. Pour the dressing over the pasta mixture and toss well. Cover and chill, if desired.

Makes 4 servings

Nutritional information per serving

Calories	589	Cal. from Fat (%)	14.7	Sodium (g)	326
Fat (g)	9.6	Saturated Fat (g)	2.8	Cholesterol (mg)	24
Protein (g)	31.4	Carbohydrate (g)	93		

Tuna Artichoke Pasta Salad

When you are in need of a last-minute salad, this attractive, delicious salad can be put together in no time.

8 ounces rotini (spiral) pasta
½ cup frozen peas
1 (14-ounce) can quartered
    artichoke hearts, drained
1 (9-ounce) can solid white
    tuna, packed in spring
    water, drained
3 Roma (plum) tomatoes,
    coarsely chopped

½ cup sliced green onions
    (scallions)
2 tablespoons grated
    Parmesan cheese
½ cup fat-free Italian
    Parmesan dressing

Cook the pasta according to package directions, omitting any oil and salt. Drain, rinse, and set aside. In a large bowl, combine the pasta, peas, artichoke hearts, tuna, tomatoes, green onions, and Parmesan. Toss with the Italian Parmesan dressing.

Makes 4 to 6 servings

Nutritional information per serving

Calories	250	Cal. from Fat (%)	6.5	Sodium (g)	364
Fat (g)	1.8	Saturated Fat (g)	0.5	Cholesterol (mg)	11
Protein (g)	16.9	Carbohydrate (g)	41.6		

Spicy Pasta Salad

The tomatoes and green chilies give this super vegetarian salad a real bite.

1 (16-ounce) package ziti
    (tubular) pasta
2 (10-ounce) cans diced
    tomatoes and green
    chilies, drained
4 cups small fresh broccoli
    florets
1 (14-ounce) can quartered
    artichoke hearts, drained

2 cups sliced mushrooms
1 bunch green onions
    (scallions), sliced
¼ cup red wine vinegar
¼ cup fat-free Italian
    dressing
½ teaspoon garlic powder

Cook the pasta according to package directions, omitting any oil and salt. Drain. In a large bowl, combine the pasta, tomatoes and chilies, broccoli, artichoke hearts, mushrooms, and green onions; mix well. Mix together the vinegar, Italian dressing, and garlic powder, and toss with the salad before serving.

Makes 8 to 10 servings

Nutritional information per serving

Calories	218	Cal. from Fat (%)	4.7	Sodium (g)	383
Fat (g)	1.1	Saturated Fat (g)	0.2	Cholesterol (mg)	0
Protein (g)	8.8	Carbohydrate (g)	44.5		

Waldorf Pasta Salad

A great choice when you're in the mood for fruit, but for something more special than a simple fruit salad.

1 (8-ounce) package rotini (spiral) pasta	1 cup chopped celery
½ cup nonfat sour cream	1 green apple, cored and chopped
¼ cup lime juice	2 medium red apples, cored and chopped
2 tablespoons sugar	½ cup chopped green onions (scallions)
⅓ cup chopped pecans, toasted	

Cook the pasta according to package directions, omitting any oil and salt. Rinse with cold water; drain. Meanwhile, in a small bowl, stir together the sour cream, lime juice, and sugar; set aside. Just before serving, in a large bowl, toss together the pasta, pecans, celery, green and red apples, and green onions. Drizzle with the dressing and toss gently to coat.

Makes 4 to 6 servings

Nutritional information per serving

Calories	274	Cal. from Fat (%)	17.3	Sodium (g)	48
Fat (g)	5.3	Saturated Fat (g)	0.5	Cholesterol (mg)	3
Protein (g)	6.6	Carbohydrate (g)	50.8		

Vermicelli Feta Salad

This simple salad is best if made ahead so the flavors have time to blend. I use lots of pepper, but you can adjust the amount to your taste. The salad is simple but tastes as though it took a lot of time to prepare.

1 (16-ounce) package
vermicelli pasta, broken
into pieces
8 ounces feta cheese,
crumbled
1 (10-ounce) package frozen
green peas, thawed
1 bunch green onions
(scallions), sliced
1 red bell pepper, seeded
and diced

1 (2¼-ounce) can ripe black
olives, drained and sliced
1 (8-ounce) bottle fat-free
Italian salad dressing
¼ cup light mayonnaise
1 tablespoon Worcestershire
sauce
3 tablespoons Dijon mustard
1 teaspoon pepper

Cook the pasta according to package directions, omitting any oil and salt. Drain and rinse. Place the pasta in a large bowl. Add the feta, peas, green onions, red pepper, and olives. In a small bowl, mix together the Italian dressing, mayonnaise, Worcestershire sauce, and mustard. Toss with the pasta and season with the pepper.

Makes 8 servings

Nutritional information per serving

Calories	389	Cal. from Fat (%)	24.7	Sodium (g)	868
Fat (g)	10.7	Saturated Fat (g)	5.1	Cholesterol (mg)	28
Protein (g)	14.3	Carbohydrate (g)	58		

Salmon Pasta Salad ♥

If you don't have time to cook the salmon, substitute a 14¾-ounce can of red salmon; however, fresh salmon takes little effort to prepare, and it's so good. Also, artichoke hearts can be used instead of the hearts of palm if desired. This sensational, colorful salad will be a treat anytime.

1 pound fresh salmon fillet	2 teaspoons dried dillweed
8 ounces rotini (spiral) pasta	½ teaspoon white pepper
⅓ cup light mayonnaise	1 cup diced celery
¾ cup nonfat plain yogurt	1 (14-ounce) can hearts of
½ teaspoon sugar	palm, drained and sliced

Preheat the oven to 325° F. Place the salmon in a shallow baking dish coated with nonstick cooking spray and bake for about 15 minutes, or until the salmon is thoroughly cooked and flakes easily. Set aside to cool. Cook the pasta according to package directions, omitting any oil and salt. Drain, rinse, and set aside. In a small bowl, mix the mayonnaise, yogurt, sugar, dillweed, and pepper. Set aside. In a large bowl, mix the celery, hearts of palm, pasta, and dressing. Remove the skin from the salmon, flake into chunks, and add to the pasta mixture, tossing gently. Chill until ready to serve.

Makes 4 to 6 servings

Nutritional information per serving

Calories	314	Cal. from Fat (%)	23.1	Sodium (g)	345
Fat (g)	8.1	Saturated Fat (g)	1.5	Cholesterol (mg)	48
Protein (g)	23.9	Carbohydrate (g)	34.7		

Chicken Peanut Pasta Salad

The peanutty flavor in the sauce makes this colorful salad a unique one. You can leave out the chicken for a meatless meal.

¼ cup reduced-fat peanut
butter
2 tablespoons reduced-
sodium soy sauce
2 tablespoons seasoned rice
vinegar
1 tablespoon sugar
⅛ teaspoon crushed red
pepper flakes
8 ounces angel hair
(capellini) pasta, broken
into pieces

1 (6-ounce) package frozen
snow pea pods
¼ cup finely sliced green
onions (scallions)
½ cup shredded peeled
carrots
2 cups cooked chopped
chicken

In a bowl, stir together the peanut butter, soy sauce, vinegar, sugar, and red pepper flakes; set aside. Meanwhile, cook the pasta according to package directions, omitting any oil and salt. Drain and rinse. Cook the snow pea pods according to package directions, omitting any salt. Drain. Combine the peanut butter sauce, pasta, pea pods, green onions, carrots, and chicken in a large bowl, tossing to combine well. Cover and refrigerate for at least 1 hour before serving.

Makes 4 servings

Nutritional information per serving

Calories	497	Cal. from Fat (%)	22.5	Sodium (g)	444
Fat (g)	12.4	Saturated Fat (g)	2.9	Cholesterol (mg)	62
Protein (g)	33.8	Carbohydrate (g)	61.5		

Greek Chicken Salad Bowl

This reminds me of a Greek chef salad. The mint gives the salad a lot of personality—be adventurous!

½ cup lemon juice, divided
1 teaspoon dried mint, divided
¾ teaspoon minced garlic, divided
2 tablespoons red wine vinegar
1½ pounds skinless, boneless chicken breasts, cut into strips
½ cup dry white wine

1 pound spinach leaves, washed, stemmed, and torn into pieces
1½ cups chopped tomato
⅓ cup chopped green onions (scallions)
1½ cups chopped peeled cucumber
Salt and pepper to taste
1 tablespoon olive oil

In a bowl, mix together ¼ cup of the lemon juice, ½ teaspoon of the mint, ¼ teaspoon of the garlic, and the vinegar. Add the chicken, toss, cover with plastic wrap, and marinate in the refrigerator at least 1 hour. Coat a large skillet with nonstick cooking spray and cook the chicken over medium-high heat until brown, turning frequently, about 5 minutes. Add the wine, reduce the heat, and simmer for 8 to 10 minutes, or until the chicken is done. Remove the chicken from the pan and refrigerate until ready to use. In a large bowl, combine the spinach, tomato, green onions, cucumber, and chicken. In a small bowl, mix together the remaining lemon juice, the remaining mint, the remaining garlic, salt and pepper, and the oil. Pour the dressing over the salad, tossing to mix well. Serve immediately.

Makes 4 to 6 servings

Nutritional information per serving

Calories	203	Cal. from Fat (%)	25.1	Sodium (g)	126
Fat (g)	5.7	Saturated Fat (g)	1.2	Cholesterol (mg)	69
Protein (g)	28.1	Carbohydrate (g)	7.4		

Mandarin Chicken Salad

This super chicken salad combined with fruit and water chestnuts and tossed with a light lemon dressing is hard to beat.

1½ pounds skinless, boneless chicken breasts, cut into chunks
1 tablespoon canola oil
4 tablespoons reduced-sodium soy sauce, divided
½ teaspoon minced garlic
¼ teaspoon ground ginger
1 cup green grapes, cut in half
1 cup chopped celery
½ cup thinly sliced green onions (scallions)

1 (11-ounce) can mandarin orange segments in water, drained
1 (8-ounce) can sliced water chestnuts, drained
1 (6-ounce) container nonfat lemon yogurt
6 cups (loosely packed) washed, stemmed, torn spinach leaves

In a bowl, combine the chicken, oil, 2 tablespoons of the soy sauce, garlic, and ginger, coating the chicken well. In a skillet coated with nonstick cooking spray, cook the chicken mixture over medium heat, about 5 to 7 minutes, until the chicken is done. Set aside and let cool. In a bowl, combine the chicken, grapes, celery, green onions, orange segments, and water chestnuts. Mix together the yogurt and the remaining soy sauce and pour over the chicken mixture. Cover and refrigerate until the mixture is well chilled, about 2 hours. Serve on the spinach leaves.

Makes 4 to 6 servings

Nutritional information per serving

Calories	253	Cal. from Fat (%)	20	Sodium (g)	467
Fat (g)	5.6	Saturated Fat (g)	1.1	Cholesterol (mg)	71
Protein (g)	29.5	Carbohydrate (g)	21.5		

Chicken Fiesta Salad

The well-seasoned chicken with the beans, cilantro, tomato, and onion tossed with a light dressing make this a colorful salad with a Southwestern personality.

1½ pounds skinless, boneless chicken breasts
1 teaspoon ground cumin
1 teaspoon chili powder
¼ cup all-purpose flour
1 (15-ounce) can pinto beans, drained and rinsed
2 cups frozen corn, thawed

1 cup chopped tomato
½ cup chopped red onion
¼ cup chopped fresh cilantro
1 tablespoon olive oil
½ teaspoon minced garlic
½ cup lime juice
¼ cup red wine vinegar

Cut the chicken into strips. In a small bowl, combine the cumin, chili powder, and flour. Coat the chicken with the flour mixture and sauté the chicken, over medium-high heat, in a large skillet coated with nonstick cooking spray until browned, about 5 minutes. Set aside. In a large bowl, combine the pinto beans, corn, tomato, red onion, and cilantro. In a small bowl, combine the oil, garlic, lime juice, and vinegar. Pour over the vegetables in a bowl. Add the chicken strips, tossing to mix together.

Makes 6 servings

Nutritional information per serving

Calories	303	Cal. from Fat (%) 18.3		Sodium (g)	187
Fat (g)	6.2	Saturated Fat (g)	1.3	Cholesterol (mg)	69
Protein (g)	31.9	Carbohydrate (g) 31.6			

Hot Chicken Salad

This is a rich-tasting warm chicken salad that can also stand in as a casserole dish. I find it perfect for a luncheon or a light evening meal.

3 cups cubed cooked
  chicken breasts
1 (10¾-ounce) can reduced-
  fat cream of mushroom
  soup
¼ cup light mayonnaise
1 cup chopped celery

¼ cup dry bread crumbs
⅛ teaspoon pepper
1 cup cooked rice
½ cup sliced green onions
  (scallions)
2 large hard-boiled eggs,
  whites only, chopped

Preheat the oven to 375° F. In a large bowl, mix together the chicken, mushroom soup, mayonnaise, celery, bread crumbs, pepper, rice, green onions, and hard-boiled egg whites. Place in a 1½-quart casserole dish coated with nonstick cooking spray. Bake, covered, for 25 minutes. Uncover and bake for 5 minutes longer.

Makes 4 servings

Nutritional information per serving

Calories	363	Cal. from Fat (%)	27	Sodium (g)	612
Fat (g)	10.9	Saturated Fat (g)	2.8	Cholesterol (mg)	101
Protein (g)	37.3	Carbohydrate (g)	25.6		

Indian Chicken Salad

The distinct flavors of curry and ginger combined with the sweetness of oranges make this salad a great way to use leftover chicken.

½ cup plain nonfat yogurt
2 tablespoons finely chopped
  red onion
Dash of cayenne pepper
Salt to taste
1 pound sweet potatoes,
  peeled and cut into 1-inch
  cubes
1 pound cooked skinless,
  boneless chicken breasts,
  cut into 1-inch chunks

1 medium peeled carrot,
  shredded
1 teaspoon curry powder
¼ teaspoon ground ginger
2 navel oranges, peeled and
  cut into segments
⅓ cup orange juice
6 cups (loosely packed)
  washed, stemmed spinach
  leaves

In a small bowl, whisk together the yogurt, red onion, cayenne, and salt. Set aside. In a medium pot, cover the sweet potatoes with water, bring to a simmer over medium heat, and cook until tender, about 10 minutes. Remove the sweet potatoes to a large bowl. Combine the chicken with the sweet potatoes and add the carrot. Stir in the curry powder, ginger, and oranges. Toss this mixture with the prepared yogurt dressing and add the orange juice to thin the dressing. Line a large bowl with the spinach leaves and top with the chicken mixture.

Makes 4 servings

Nutritional information per serving

Calories	369	Cal. from Fat (%) 11.7	Sodium (g)	161
Fat (g)	4.8	Saturated Fat (g) 1.3	Cholesterol (mg)	97
Protein (g)	40.8	Carbohydrate (g) 40.4		

Smoked Turkey and Wild Rice Salad ♥

When you're lucky enough to get a smoked turkey for a present, here's a sensational and sophisticated salad to make with the leftovers. You can also make it with baked turkey.

4 cups cooked wild rice
1½ cups coarsely chopped cooked smoked turkey breast
1 cup coarsely chopped Roma (plum) tomatoes
½ cup chopped green bell pepper
½ cup chopped green onions (scallions)
¼ cup chopped parsley
¼ cup balsamic vinegar
1 tablespoon canola oil
½ teaspoon ground ginger
½ teaspoon minced garlic
Lettuce leaves

In a large bowl, combine the cooked wild rice, turkey, tomatoes, green pepper, green onions, and parsley. In another small bowl, combine the vinegar, oil, ginger, and garlic, mixing vigorously. Pour over the turkey mixture and toss well. Spoon the salad onto a large serving platter lined with lettuce leaves.

Makes 6 servings

Nutritional information per serving

Calories	193	Cal. from Fat (%) 14.6	Sodium (g)	27
Fat (g)	3.1	Saturated Fat (g) 0.3	Cholesterol (mg)	29
Protein (g)	15.5	Carbohydrate (g) 26.8		

Shrimp and Rice Salad

What presentation and what flavor! It's so simple to make, but everyone will come back for seconds.

1 (16-ounce) can fat-free chicken broth
1 bay leaf
1 cup rice
½ pound medium shrimp, peeled
½ cup sliced green onions (scallions)

⅓ cup thinly sliced radishes
1 cup frozen peas, thawed
1 teaspoon dried dillweed
⅔ cup nonfat sour cream
¼ cup light mayonnaise
1 tablespoon lemon juice

In a 2-quart saucepan over high heat, heat the chicken broth and bay leaf to boiling. Stir in the rice and reduce the heat to low. Cover and simmer for 10 minutes. Add the shrimp to the rice mixture, cover, and continue cooking over low heat, 10 to 15 minutes more, or until the liquid is absorbed and the shrimp turn pink. Set aside to cool. In a medium bowl, combine the green onions, radishes, peas, dillweed, sour cream, mayonnaise, and lemon juice with the rice mixture. Cover and refrigerate for 2 hours, or until serving time.

Makes 4 to 6 servings

Nutritional information per serving

Calories	241	Cal. from Fat (%) 15.1	Sodium (g)	392
Fat (g)	4.1	Saturated Fat (g) 0.8	Cholesterol (mg)	62
Protein (g)	11.4	Carbohydrate (g) 36.9		

Wild Rice and Pork Salad

This is a great way to use up leftover meat, or for an extra-tasty salad, use teriyaki or peppered pork tenderloins, which are available in your grocery store.

2 (6-ounce) packages long-grain and wild rice
1 (6-ounce) package frozen snow pea pods
1 (8-ounce) can sliced water chestnuts, drained
1 (11-ounce) can mandarin orange segments in water, drained

2 cups chopped cooked pork tenderloin (about 1¼ pounds)
¼ cup low-sodium soy sauce
¼ cup seasoned rice vinegar
2 tablespoons olive oil
1 teaspoon ground ginger

Prepare the rice according to package directions, omitting any oil and salt; set aside. Prepare the pea pods according to package directions; set aside. In a large bowl, combine the cooked rice, pea pods, water chestnuts, oranges, and pork, tossing well. In a small bowl, whisk together the soy sauce, vinegar, oil, and ginger. Pour over the rice salad and gently toss. Cover and refrigerate for at least 2 hours.

Makes 6 to 8 servings

Nutritional information per serving

Calories	389	Cal. from Fat (%) 16.9		Sodium (g)	1,000
Fat (g)	7.3	Saturated Fat (g) 1.6		Cholesterol (mg)	42
Protein (g)	23.3	Carbohydrate (g) 57.9			

Tropical Shrimp Salad

Now that precut melon and pineapple are readily available in supermarkets, this refreshing salad couldn't be easier to whip up. Just serve it on plates instead of in the melon shells.

2 small honeydew melons or
  cantaloupes, chilled
1 pound fresh pineapple
  chunks
1 cup thinly sliced peeled
  cucumber (about 1 small)
1 pound medium shrimp,
  cooked and peeled

⅓ cup plain nonfat yogurt
2 tablespoons light
  mayonnaise
½ teaspoon dried dillweed
1 teaspoon sugar
½ teaspoon grated lemon
  rind
1 tablespoon lemon juice

Cut each melon in half and remove the seeds and pulp. Scoop the melon flesh from each half, and chop, leaving a 1-inch-thick shell. Mix the pineapple chunks, chopped melon, cucumber, and shrimp together in a large bowl. In a small bowl, combine the yogurt, mayonnaise, dillweed, sugar, lemon rind, and lemon juice and then mix with the shrimp mixture. Spoon a fourth of the filling into each shell. Serve immediately.

Makes 4 servings

Nutritional information per serving

Calories	349	Cal. from Fat (%) 11.3		Sodium (g)	292
Fat (g)	4.4	Saturated Fat (g) 0.8		Cholesterol (mg)	149
Protein (g)	19.7	Carbohydrate (g) 64			

Paella Salad

This attractive salad of many colors and textures will convince even the heartiest eaters that a salad can make a satisfying meal.

2 (5-ounce) packages saffron yellow rice
¼ cup balsamic vinegar
¼ cup lemon juice
1 tablespoon olive oil
1 teaspoon dried basil
⅛ teaspoon pepper
Dash of cayenne pepper
1 pound medium shrimp, peeled and cooked
1 (14-ounce) can quartered artichoke hearts, drained

¾ cup chopped green bell pepper
1 cup frozen green peas, thawed
1 cup chopped tomato
1 (2-ounce) jar diced pimientos, drained
½ cup chopped red onion
2 ounces chopped prosciutto

Prepare the rice according to package directions, omitting any oil and salt. Set aside. In a small bowl, mix together the vinegar, lemon juice, oil, basil, pepper, and cayenne; set aside. In a large bowl, combine the cooked rice with the shrimp, artichoke hearts, green pepper, peas, tomato, pimientos, red onion, and prosciutto, mixing well. Pour the dressing over the rice mixture, tossing to coat. Cover and refrigerate at least 2 hours before serving.

Makes 6 servings

Nutritional information per serving

Calories	325	Cal. from Fat (%)	10.8	Sodium (g)	1,277
Fat (g)	3.9	Saturated Fat (g)	0.7	Cholesterol (mg)	152
Protein (g)	24.3	Carbohydrate (g)	48.8		

Poached Salmon
with Creamy Potato Salad

The salmon and the potato salad are super recipes individually. When you put them together with the tomatoes, you have a truly spectacular presentation. Poaching the salmon really is an easy procedure, so give this recipe a try.

2 pounds salmon fillets	⅔ cup nonfat sour cream
½ cup balsamic vinegar	1 tablespoon lemon juice
½ teaspoon sugar	1 (2-ounce) jar diced
1½ teaspoons dried	pimientos, drained
dillweed, divided	1 teaspoon dry mustard
⅛ teaspoon hot pepper	Salt and pepper to taste
sauce	2 cups sliced Roma (plum)
2 pounds red potatoes	tomatoes

Preheat the oven to 350°F. Arrange the salmon fillets, skin side down, in a 2-quart oblong baking dish coated with nonstick cooking spray. In a small bowl, combine the vinegar, the sugar, ½ teaspoon of the dillweed, and the hot sauce. Pour over the salmon and bake for about 20 minutes, or until the salmon is done and flakes with a fork. Remove the skin and any bones. Chill until ready to serve. Place the potatoes in a medium-size pot, cover with water, and bring to a boil. Reduce the heat and simmer for 20 to 25 minutes, or until the potatoes are tender. Drain, let cool, and slice into quarters. In a small bowl, mix together the sour cream, lemon juice, pimientos, remaining dillweed, mustard, and salt and pepper. Combine the dressing with the potatoes in a large bowl, tossing to coat. Cover and refrigerate at least 2 hours. To serve, place the salmon in the center of a serving platter. Place the sliced tomatoes and potato salad around the salmon.

Makes 6 servings

Nutritional information per serving

Calories	369	Cal. from Fat (%) 14.9		Sodium (g)	170
Fat (g)	6.1	Saturated Fat (g)	1	Cholesterol (mg)	90
Protein (g)	37.3	Carbohydrate (g) 39.6			

Chicken Kiwi Salad

You'll wish for leftover chicken just so you can make this Asian-influenced recipe. The kiwi gives this salad the color, the water chestnuts give it the crunch, and the dressing makes it so flavorful!

¼ cup lime juice
2 tablespoons honey
2 tablespoons reduced-sodium soy sauce
½ teaspoon ground ginger
2 pounds cooked skinless, boneless chicken breasts, sliced

4 kiwis, peeled and thinly sliced
1 (8-ounce) can sliced water chestnuts, drained
¼ cup chopped red onion
8 cups (loosely packed) washed torn romaine lettuce

In a small bowl, combine the lime juice, honey, soy sauce, and ginger. Pour ⅓ cup of this dressing (set the remaining dresing aside) over the cooked chicken slices in a large bowl and set aside to marinate for at least 1 hour. Then mix the kiwis, water chestnuts, and red onion with the marinated chicken slices. Line a serving bowl with the romaine lettuce. Combine the chicken mixture and remaining dressing with the lettuce, tossing gently.

Makes 4 servings

Nutritional information per serving

Calories	507	Cal. from Fat (%) 15.5	Sodium (g)	458
Fat (g)	8.7	Saturated Fat (g) 2.3	Cholesterol (mg)	193
Protein (g)	73.9	Carbohydrate (g) 30.8		

POULTRY

Chunky Chicken Divan

I thought this recipe would be great for those who don't like plain broccoli. It is very easy to eat, and chicken and broccoli always seem to team up to make a winner.

2 pounds skinless, boneless
  chicken breasts
Salt and pepper to taste
2 (10-ounce) packages
  frozen chopped broccoli
¼ cup all-purpose flour

1½ cups skim milk
1 cup shredded reduced-fat
  Monterey Jack cheese
1 (2-ounce) jar chopped
  pimientos, drained
Paprika

Preheat the oven to 350° F. Place the chicken in a large saucepan with water to cover. Season the water with salt and pepper. Bring to a boil, reduce the heat, and simmer for about 30 minutes, or until the chicken is tender. Cut into chunks and set aside. Meanwhile, cook the broccoli according to package directions, omitting any salt. Drain and place along the bottom of a 2-quart oblong baking dish coated with nonstick cooking spray. Sprinkle with salt and pepper to taste. Put the flour in a saucepan and gradually whisk in the milk over medium heat, stirring, until thickened. Add the Monterey Jack, stirring, until the cheese is melted. Remove from the heat, add the pimientos, and season with salt and pepper. Spread the chicken chunks evenly over the broccoli. Pour the sauce evenly over the chicken and sprinkle with paprika. Bake, uncovered, about 20 minutes, or until the mixture is bubbly and heated through.

Makes 4 to 6 servings

Nutritional information per serving

Calories	293	Cal. from Fat (%)	24.1	Sodium (g)	285
Fat (g)	7.8	Saturated Fat (g)	3.8	Cholesterol (mg)	104
Protein (g)	43.4	Carbohydrate (g)	11.9		

Chicken and Broccoli Casserole

This variation of Chicken Divan will be a popular family request!

2 pounds skinless, boneless
chicken breasts, cut into
1½-inch chunks
2 (10-ounce) packages
frozen broccoli spears,
thawed
1 (10¾-ounce) can reduced-
fat cream of mushroom
soup

½ cup skim milk
1 cup shredded reduced-fat
Monterey Jack cheese
2 cups packaged cornbread
stuffing

Preheat the oven to 350° F. Coat a 3-quart casserole dish with non-stick cooking spray. Place the chicken in the dish. Top with the broccoli spears (place the broccoli spears in the dish so the stems will be in the middle with the florets on the sides of the casserole). In a small bowl, mix together the cream of mushroom soup, milk, and cheese. Spoon this mixture evenly over the broccoli layer. Top with the cornbread stuffing to cover completely. Bake, uncovered, for 50 to 60 minutes, or until the chicken is done and the casserole is bubbly.

Makes 6 servings

Nutritional information per serving

Calories	368	Cal. from Fat (%)	24.3	Sodium (g)	721
Fat (g)	9.9	Saturated Fat (g)	4.4	Cholesterol (mg)	111
Protein (g)	44.1	Carbohydrate (g)	24.9		

Ginger Chicken and Black Beans

This chicken baked with ginger, peaches, and black beans has an incredible flavor. If you prefer dark meat, just add some skinless, boneless thighs. Don't skip this recipe!

2½ pounds skinless, boneless
chicken breasts
Salt and pepper to taste
½ teaspoon garlic powder
1 teaspoon paprika
1 (15-ounce) can light sliced
peaches, drained and cut
into chunks

1 teaspoon ground ginger
2 tablespoons lime juice
1 teaspoon minced garlic
½ cup chopped green onions
(scallions)
2 (15-ounce) cans black
beans, undrained

Preheat the oven to 350° F. Place the chicken in a 2-quart oblong baking dish. Season with the salt and pepper, garlic powder, and paprika. In a bowl, combine the peaches, ginger, lime juice, garlic, green onions, and black beans. Spoon this mixture over the chicken, cover, and bake for 45 to 60 minutes, or until the chicken is tender.

Makes 6 servings

Nutritional information per serving

Calories	376	Cal. from Fat (%) 14.5		Sodium (g)	543
Fat (g)	6.1	Saturated Fat (g)	1.4	Cholesterol (mg)	116
Protein (g)	49.5	Carbohydrate (g)	28.4		

Chicken and Potatoes Picante

This is a great dish to disguise leftover chicken. Throw it all in the skillet and you have a smothered Mexican delight!

1 onion, chopped
1 green bell pepper, seeded
and chopped
1 teaspoon minced garlic
4 cups cooked peeled potato
chunks (about 2 baking
potatoes)

3 cups diced cooked skinless
chicken
1¼ cups picante sauce, plus
more if desired
Salt and pepper to taste
1 cup shredded reduced-fat
Monterey Jack cheese

In a large skillet coated with nonstick cooking spray, sautè the onion and green pepper over medium heat until tender, stirring, about 5 minutes. Add the garlic, potatoes, chicken, picante sauce, and salt and pepper and toss gently. Simmer 5 minutes, stirring occasionally. Top with the Monterey Jack, cover, and simmer until the cheese is melted. Serve with additional picante sauce, if desired.

Makes 6 servings

Nutritional information per serving

Calories	286	Cal. from Fat (%) 29.4		Sodium (g)	553
Fat (g)	9.4	Saturated Fat (g) 4.1		Cholesterol (mg)	76
Protein (g)	26.9	Carbohydrate (g) 23.2			

Rich and Creamy Chicken and Potatoes

For those who think the richer the better, check out this dish. Sprinkle the top of the chicken with chopped parsley for a little color.

3 pounds skinless, boneless chicken breasts
1 (10¾-ounce) can reduced-fat cream of chicken soup
1 (8-ounce) package fat-free cream cheese, softened
1 (8-ounce) container nonfat sour cream
3 pounds baking potatoes, peeled and cut into chunks
3 tablespoons light stick margarine
1 cup skim milk
1 teaspoon minced garlic
1 bunch green onions (scallions), chopped

Preheat the oven to 350° F. Place the chicken in a 3-quart casserole dish coated with nonstick cooking spray. In a bowl, combine the cream of chicken soup, cream cheese, and sour cream, mixing well. Pour over the chicken breasts, turning to coat. Cover with foil and bake for 1 hour to 1 hour and 10 minutes, or until the chicken is done. Meanwhile, place the potatoes in a saucepan with water to cover. Bring to a boil, reduce heat, and cook until the potatoes are tender, about 15 minutes. Remove the potatoes from the heat, place in a bowl, and mash. Blend in the margarine, milk, garlic, and green onions until the potatoes are creamy. Serve the chicken and sauce over the creamed potatoes.

Makes 8 servings

Nutritional information per serving

Calories	457	Cal. from Fat (%) 16.3		Sodium (g)	487
Fat (g)	8.3	Saturated Fat (g) 2.2		Cholesterol (mg)	117
Protein (g)	17.7	Carbohydrate (g) 45.2			

Chicken Pot Pie ♥

I always get excited when I prepare this recipe, because it looks just as perfect as the commercially prepared ones but it tastes so much better! Use leftover chicken and impress your family.

1 cup diced peeled carrot
1 cup sliced mushrooms
½ cup chopped celery
½ cup frozen peas, thawed
¼ cup finely chopped onion
¼ cup all-purpose flour
1 (12-ounce) can evaporated
 skimmed milk

2 cups diced cooked skinless,
 boneless chicken breasts
½ teaspoon pepper
½ teaspoon dried thyme
1 cup self-rising flour
1½ tablespoons light stick
 margarine
½ cup skim milk

Preheat the oven to 450° F. Coat a large skillet with nonstick cooking spray and place over medium-high heat. Add the carrots, mushrooms, celery, peas, and onion and sauté 5 minutes, or until the vegetables are tender. Add the all-purpose flour, stirring, and gradually add the evaporated milk, stirring until the mixture thickens. Stir in the chicken, pepper, and thyme. Transfer the mixture into a 9-inch pie plate coated with nonstick cooking spray. Place the self-rising flour in a small bowl; cut in the margarine with a pastry blender or two knives until the mixture is crumbly. Gradually add the skim milk, a little at a time, evenly over the flour, stirring with a fork until the dry ingredients are moistened. Drop the dough evenly by spoonfuls onto the chicken mixture. Bake, uncovered, for 15 to 20 minutes, or until the crust is golden.

Makes 6 servings

Nutritional information per serving

Calories	270	Cal. from Fat (%) 14.2		Sodium (g)	440
Fat (g)	4.2	Saturated Fat (g)	1	Cholesterol (mg)	42
Protein (g)	23.8	Carbohydrate (g) 33.1			

Creamy Chicken and Spinach

This creamy spinach topped with chicken and cheese will easily satisfy your taste for a rich dish. It's great with leftover chicken, or leave out the chicken for a wonderful vegetable side dish.

½ pound mushrooms, sliced
1 onion, chopped
1 teaspoon minced garlic
1 (8-ounce) package fat-free cream cheese
1 cup skim milk
2 (10-ounce) packages frozen chopped spinach, thawed and squeezed dry

2 cups cooked cubed chicken breasts
1 cup shredded reduced-fat Monterey Jack cheese

Preheat the oven to 350° F. In a large skillet coated with nonstick cooking spray, sauté the mushrooms, onion, and garlic over medium heat until tender, about 3 to 5 minutes. Blend in the cream cheese and gradually add the milk, mashing with a spoon until the cream cheese is melted. Stir in the spinach. Transfer the spinach mixture into a 1½-quart casserole dish coated with nonstick cooking spray. Top with the cooked chicken and sprinkle with the Monterey Jack. Bake for 10 minutes, uncovered, or until the cheese is melted and the dish is heated throughout.

Makes 4 to 6 servings

Nutritional information per serving

Calories	217	Cal. from Fat (%)	25.4	Sodium (g)	464
Fat (g)	6.1	Saturated Fat (g)	3.3	Cholesterol (mg)	58
Protein (g)	29.3	Carbohydrate (g)	12.7		

Chicken Florentine

This attractive casserole has a light lemon flavor. You can use cooked skinless, boneless chicken breasts instead of different pieces of the chicken if you prefer. The dish freezes well.

1 (10-ounce) package frozen chopped spinach
¼ cup all-purpose flour
1 cup skim milk
1 cup canned fat-free chicken broth
8 ounces wide noodles
2 cups nonfat sour cream
⅓ cup lemon juice
1 (8-ounce) can mushroom stems and pieces, drained
1 (8-ounce) can sliced water chestnuts, drained
1 (2-ounce) jar diced pimientos, drained
1 large onion, chopped
½ teaspoon cayenne pepper
1 teaspoon paprika
Salt and pepper to taste
2 whole chickens, about 2½ to 3 pounds each, cooked, skinned, deboned, and chopped
1½ cups shredded reduced-fat Cheddar cheese

Cook the spinach according to package directions, omitting any salt. Preheat the oven to 350° F. In a large pot, blend the flour, milk, and chicken broth. Cook over low heat, stirring continuously, until thickened. Meanwhile, prepare the noodles according to package directions, omitting any oil and salt. Drain. Add the noodles, sour cream, lemon juice, cooked spinach, mushrooms, water chestnuts, pimiento, onion, cayenne pepper, paprika, and salt and pepper to the thickened broth. In a 3-quart oblong baking dish coated with nonstick cooking spray, alternate layers of the noodle mixture and chicken. Top with the cheese and bake, uncovered, for 30 minutes, or until bubbly.

Makes 12 servings

Nutritional information per serving

Calories	411	Cal. from Fat (%)	26.8	Sodium (g)	398
Fat (g)	12.2	Saturated Fat (g)	4.5	Cholesterol (mg)	132
Protein (g)	41.8	Carbohydrate (g)	29.1		

Polynesian Chicken

The preserves combined with the barbecue sauce give the sauce that spicy-sweet flavor. This dish is like taking a trip to the South Pacific, only faster and much less expensive!

2 pounds skinless, boneless chicken breasts, cut into strips
⅓ cup all-purpose flour
Salt and pepper to taste
1 (16-ounce) jar peach preserves
⅔ cup barbecue sauce
1 cup coarsely chopped onions

3 tablespoons reduced-sodium soy sauce
1 (8-ounce) can sliced water chestnuts, drained
1 large green bell pepper, seeded and cut into strips
4 cups cooked rice

Coat the chicken with the flour and salt and pepper. In a large skillet coated with nonstick cooking spray, brown the chicken over medium-high heat, about 5 minutes. In a bowl, combine the preserves, barbecue sauce, onions, and soy sauce. Pour over the chicken. Cover and simmer for 30 to 40 minutes. Add the water chestnuts and green pepper, and continue cooking for 10 minutes more. Serve over the rice.

Makes 6 servings

Nutritional information per serving

Calories	593	Cal. from Fat (%)	7.6	Sodium (g)	641
Fat (g)	5	Saturated Fat (g)	1.3	Cholesterol (mg)	93
Protein (g)	39.7	Carbohydrate (g)	97.8		

Tarragon Chicken with Carrots

This chicken has a creamy sauce that is deceptively rich. Tarragon and chicken are a classic pairing.

2 pounds skinless, boneless
  chicken breasts
1 teaspoon dried tarragon
Salt and pepper to taste
1 tablespoon light stick
  margarine
1 cup sliced peeled carrots
1 bunch green onions
  (scallions), sliced

⅔ cup dry white wine
½ cup nonfat sour cream
1 tablespoon all-purpose
  flour
4 cups cooked rice
1 tablespoon chopped
  parsley

Season the chicken with the tarragon and salt and pepper. In a large skillet coated with nonstick cooking spray, melt the margarine and sauté the chicken breasts over medium heat until brown, about 5 to 10 minutes. Remove the chicken and sauté the carrots and green onions in the pan drippings, about 5 minutes. Add the wine, sour cream, and flour. Return the chicken to the pan and continue cooking, covered, for 20 minutes longer, or until the chicken is done. Mix the rice with the parsley and serve with the chicken.

Makes 4 to 6 servings

Nutritional information per serving

Calories	395	Cal. from Fat (%)	13.2	Sodium (g)	143
Fat (g)	5.8	Saturated Fat (g)	1.4	Cholesterol (mg)	96
Protein (g)	38.7	Carbohydrate (g)	39.5		

Simple Chicken Combo

It's amazing how only five ingredients make a great dinner that the kids will even enjoy. The salsa gives the dish a bite and some nice color.

1½ pounds skinless, boneless
  chicken, cut into 1½-inch
  chunks
1 (16-ounce) jar salsa
2 (14½-ounce) cans fat-free
  chicken broth

2 cups rice
1 (16-ounce) package frozen
  corn

In a large pot coated with nonstick cooking spray, cook the chicken pieces over medium heat until they are slightly browned, about 8 minutes. Add the salsa and chicken broth and bring to a boil. Add the rice and corn, lower the heat, cover, and cook until the liquid is absorbed and the rice is done, about 20 to 25 minutes.

Makes 8 servings

Nutritional information per serving

Calories	365	Cal. from Fat (%)	7.4	Sodium (g)	681
Fat (g)	3	Saturated Fat (g)	0.8	Cholesterol (mg)	52
Protein (g)	25.4	Carbohydrate (g)	57.1		

Italian Chicken

This is way too easy to be so good! The Italian herbs give that finishing touch.

1½ cups water
1 cup rice
1 (10-ounce) can diced
tomatoes and green
chilies, drained
½ cup chopped onion
½ cup shredded part-skim
mozzarella cheese
2 teaspoons dried basil,
divided

2 teaspoons dried oregano,
divided
1 teaspoon minced garlic
1½ pounds skinless, boneless
chicken breasts, cut into
strips
¼ cup grated Parmesan
cheese

Preheat the oven to 375° F. In a 2- to 3-quart oblong baking dish coated with nonstick cooking spray, combine the water, rice, tomatoes and chilies, onion, mozzarella, 1 teaspoon of the basil, 1 teaspoon of the oregano, and the garlic, stirring well. Top the rice mixture with the chicken strips and sprinkle with the remaining basil and oregano and the Parmesan. Bake, covered, for 45 minutes. Uncover and continue baking 15 minutes longer, or until the chicken is tender and the rice is cooked.

Makes 4 servings

Nutritional information per serving

Calories	469	Cal. from Fat (%)	16.7	Sodium (g)	539
Fat (g)	8.7	Saturated Fat (g)	3.8	Cholesterol (mg)	116
Protein (g)	48.3	Carbohydrate (g)	46.2		

Sweet-and-Sour Chicken, Potatoes, and Spinach

A tangy sauce makes this chicken dish a little different. Since the spinach is fresh, add it at the end and stir only until wilted.

5 medium-size red potatoes
(about 1¼ pounds)
1 bell pepper, seeded and
cut into ½-inch strips
(preferably yellow)
1 tablespoon minced garlic
1 pound mushrooms, halved
2 pounds skinless, boneless
chicken breasts, cut into
chunks

2 tablespoons light brown
sugar
3 tablespoons balsamic
vinegar
3 tablespoons reduced-
sodium soy sauce
1 (10-ounce) bag fresh
spinach, washed, stemmed,
and torn into pieces

Cut each unpeeled potato into quarters. Place the potatoes in a 3-quart saucepan, add enough water to cover, and bring the potatoes to a boil over high heat. Reduce the heat to low, cover, and simmer 10 to 15 minutes, or until the potatoes are tender. Drain. In a skillet coated with nonstick cooking spray, sauté the pepper, garlic, and mushrooms over a high heat, stirring frequently, until crisp-tender, about 5 minutes. Remove from the skillet and set aside. In the same skillet recoated with nonstick cooking spray, cook the chicken over medium heat until browned, about 5 minutes. Return the vegetables to the skillet. Cover, reduce the heat to medium, and cook for 15 minutes longer, or until the chicken is tender. Meanwhile, in a cup, stir together the brown sugar, vinegar, and soy sauce. When the chicken is done, increase the heat to high and add the potatoes and vinegar mixture. Then stir in the spinach, a little at a time, cooking just until it begins to wilt.

Makes 6 servings

Nutritional information per serving

Calories	335	Cal. from Fat (%) 12.3	Sodium (g)	428
Fat (g)	4.6	Saturated Fat (g) 1.2	Cholesterol (mg)	93
Protein (g)	39.7	Carbohydrate (g) 34.5		

Chicken Creole

The browned flour serves as a thickening agent and enhances the flavor of the dish. By browning the flour in the oven instead of a skillet, the need for any oil is eliminated.

1 cup all-purpose flour
1 large onion, chopped
1 green bell pepper, seeded and chopped
$\frac{1}{2}$ pound mushrooms, sliced
$\frac{1}{2}$ cup chopped celery
1 cup chopped green onion (scallions)
$\frac{1}{2}$ cup chopped parsley
1 tablespoon minced garlic
2 (15-ounce) cans no-salt-added tomato sauce

1 ($14\frac{1}{2}$-ounce) can no-salt-added whole tomatoes, chopped, with their juices
$\frac{1}{2}$ cup dry white wine
1 tablespoon Worcestershire sauce
4 pounds skinless, boneless chicken breasts, cut into 2-inch pieces
6 cups cooked rice

Preheat the oven to 375° F. Spread the flour evenly on a baking sheet and cook in the oven for 30 minutes, or until medium brown in color, stirring occasionally. Set aside. In a large pot coated with nonstick cooking spray, sauté the onion, green pepper, mushrooms, celery, and green onions until tender, about 5 minutes. Add the parsley and garlic. Add the browned flour, stirring. Gradually add the tomato sauce, tomatoes, wine, and Worcestershire sauce, stirring, until the flour is well mixed. Add the chicken pieces. Bring to a boil, reduce the heat, and cook, covered, for 45 minutes. You may need to add water if it becomes too thick. Serve over the cooked rice.

Makes 8 servings

Nutritional information per serving

Calories	551	Cal. from Fat (%)	10.7	Sodium (g)	179
Fat (g)	6.6	Saturated Fat (g)	1.8	Cholesterol (mg)	139
Protein (g)	59	Carbohydrate (g)	58.1		

Chicken Rice Stir-Fry

This super Chinese chicken dish is very tasty and faster than take-out!

2 large egg whites
2 tablespoons dry sherry
1 tablespoon cornstarch
Salt and pepper to taste
1½ pounds skinless, boneless
    chicken breasts, cut into
    strips
1 teaspoon ground ginger
1 teaspoon minced garlic

6 green onions (scallions),
    cut into ½-inch lengths
3 cups peeled carrot strips
1½ cups rice
3 cups canned fat-free
    chicken broth
2 tablespoons reduced-
    sodium soy sauce
3 cups broccoli florets

In a medium bowl, beat the egg whites, sherry, cornstarch, and salt and pepper until smooth. Add the chicken and stir to coat. In a large skillet coated with nonstick cooking spray, heat the ginger and garlic over medium heat, add the chicken, and stir-fry until the chicken is lightly browned, about 5 to 8 minutes. Transfer the chicken to a plate and set aside. Add the green onions, carrots, rice, chicken broth, and soy sauce to the skillet. Cover, reduce the heat to low, and simmer for 10 minutes. Return the chicken to the skillet, add the broccoli, cover, and simmer until the rice is tender and the chicken is done, about 15 to 20 minutes longer.

Makes 4 to 6 servings

Nutritional information per serving

Calories	395	Cal. from Fat (%)	8.3	Sodium (g)	596
Fat (g)	3.6	Saturated Fat (g)	1	Cholesterol (mg)	69
Protein (g)	33.9	Carbohydrate (g)	53		

Chicken-Vegetable Stroganoff

What flavor and what color this dish has! This is a favorite with all my friends.

¼ cup Marsala wine
½ cup nonfat sour cream
2 tablespoons Dijon mustard
1½ pounds skinless, boneless chicken breasts, cut into strips
¼ teaspoon crushed red pepper flakes
1 teaspoon minced garlic
2 cups sliced peeled carrots

1 medium onion, sliced, and separated into rings
1 pound mushrooms, sliced
1 tablespoon reduced-sodium soy sauce
2 tablespoons all-purpose flour
1 (16-ounce) package wide noodles

Combine the marsala, sour cream, and mustard in a small bowl. Set aside. In a large skillet coated with nonstick cooking spray, cook the chicken until lightly browned, about 7 minutes. Remove the chicken from the skillet and set aside. Add the crushed red pepper, garlic, carrots, and onion to the skillet and sauté for 5 minutes, or until the vegetables are tender. Return the chicken to the skillet. Add the mushrooms, soy sauce, and flour. Cover and simmer 5 to 10 minutes, until the mushrooms are tender. Stir in the sour cream mixture and cook only until heated through. Meanwhile, cook the noodles according to package directions, omitting any oil and salt. Drain. Serve the chicken and vegetables over the noodles.

Makes 6 servings

Nutritional information per serving

Calories	493	Cal. from Fat (%)	12.1	Sodium (g)	285
Fat (g)	6.6	Saturated Fat (g)	1.6	Cholesterol (mg)	138
Protein (g)	38.4	Carbohydrate (g)	65.7		

Roasted Stuffed Chicken and Vegetables

When this dish comes out of the oven, get the camera ready! Nothing is better than roasted chicken and vegetables. The mashed potatoes are a great alternative for stuffing the chicken.

1 whole roasting chicken
  (5½ to 6 pounds)
Salt and pepper to taste
1½ teaspoons garlic powder
1 teaspoon dried thyme
Potato Stuffing (recipe
  follows)

1 pound medium carrots,
  peeled and cut into 1-inch
  lengths
1 onion, thinly sliced
1 (16-ounce) package frozen
  Brussels sprouts, thawed
  and drained

Preheat the oven to 350° F. Sprinkle the chicken with the salt and pepper, garlic powder, and thyme. Place the chicken, breast side up, in a medium roasting pan. Stuff the chicken with the Potato Stuffing. Roast, uncovered, for 1 hour. Skim the excess fat from the drippings, then scatter the carrots and onion around the chicken. Roast, uncovered, 15 minutes more and add the Brussels sprouts to the pan. Continue roasting the chicken, uncovered, 40 minutes more, or until the chicken is done and the vegetables are tender. Remove the skin before serving.

Makes 6 servings

Potato Stuffing

2 pounds baking potatoes,
  peeled, cooked, and
  mashed
1 teaspoon minced garlic
¼ cup skim milk

Salt and pepper to taste
2 tablespoons chopped
  parsley
⅓ cup chopped green onions
  (scallions)

In a large bowl, mix the potatoes, garlic, milk, salt and pepper, parsley, and green onions. If there is any remaining stuffing after stuffing the chicken, save it for another meal.

Nutritional information per serving

Calories	447	Cal. from Fat (%)	22.1	Sodium (g)	170
Fat (g)	11	Saturated Fat (g)	3	Cholesterol (mg)	118
Protein (g)	45.7	Carbohydrate (g)	41.8		

Cranberry Chicken with Wild Rice

This great holiday dish is pretty on the plate, and the cranberry sauce with a touch of orange liqueur makes it the perfect combination with the wild rice.

1 (16-ounce) can whole-berry cranberry sauce

2 tablespoons orange liqueur

2 tablespoons lemon juice

½ teaspoon dry mustard

1½ pounds skinless, boneless chicken breasts

1 (6-ounce) package long-grain and wild rice

2 tablespoons grated orange rind

Preheat the oven to 350° F. In a medium saucepan over medium heat, combine the cranberry sauce, orange liqueur, lemon juice, and mustard, cooking until hot. Place the chicken in a baking dish and pour the cranberry sauce over the chicken. Bake, uncovered, for 45 minutes. Meanwhile, cook the wild rice according to the package directions, omitting any oil and salt. When the rice is done, stir in the orange rind. To serve, place the rice on a plate and top with the chicken and cranberry sauce.

Makes 6 servings

Nutritional information per serving

Calories	400	Cal. from Fat (%)	9.3	Sodium (g)	413
Fat (g)	4.1	Saturated Fat (g)	1	Cholesterol (mg)	87
Protein (g)	35	Carbohydrate (g)	53.8		

Smothered Chicken

If you're a chicken à la king fan or pot pie fan, this simple dish will win you over. All the vegetables cooked together become part of the flavorful sauce. If you like dark meat, you can use skinless thighs or a combination of breasts and thighs.

2 pounds skinless, boneless chicken breasts
Salt and pepper to taste
1½ cups halved mushrooms
1 (14½-ounce) can fat-free chicken broth
½ cup chopped green bell pepper
½ cup chopped celery

¼ cup sliced green onions (scallions)
½ teaspoon dried thyme
¼ cup skim milk
3 tablespoons all-purpose flour
1 (8-ounce) package fettuccine pasta

In a large skillet coated with nonstick cooking spray, cook the chicken breasts until lightly browned, about 10 minutes. Season with salt and pepper. Remove the chicken from the skillet; set aside. In the same skillet, stir together the mushrooms, chicken broth, green pepper, celery, green onions, and thyme. Bring to a boil, scraping up the browned bits from the bottom of the skillet. Return the chicken to the skillet. Bring to a boil, reduce the heat, cover, and simmer about 20 to 25 minutes, or until the chicken is tender. In a small bowl, stir together the milk and flour until smooth. Stir into the juices in the skillet. Cook, stirring, until thickened and bubbly, about 5 minutes. Meanwhile, prepare the pasta according to package directions, omitting any oil and salt. Drain. Serve the chicken and vegetables over the pasta.

Makes 4 to 6 servings

Nutritional information per serving

Calories	353	Cal. from Fat (%) 12.1	Sodium (g)	257
Fat (g)	4.7	Saturated Fat (g) 1.2	Cholesterol (mg)	93
Protein (g)	40.4	Carbohydrate (g) 34.2		

Orange-Glazed Cornish Hens with Rice Stuffing

POULTRY

These hens make a spectacular presentation. The orange flavor enhances the stuffing and hens, and the glaze gives them a beautiful brown color. A perfect holiday dish!

1 cup chopped onion
1 green bell pepper, seeded and chopped
2 ounces Canadian bacon, finely chopped
1 large orange, peeled, seeded, and coarsely chopped

3 cups cooked rice
6 (1½-pound) Cornish hens
1 (14½-ounce) can fat-free chicken broth
½ cup orange juice
⅓ cup honey
¼ cup cornstarch

Preheat the oven to 375° F. In a medium skillet coated with nonstick cooking spray, sauté the onion, green pepper, and bacon over medium-high heat until the onion is tender, about 5 minutes. Remove from the heat and mix in the oranges pieces and rice. Rinse the hens with cold water and pat dry. Stuff each of the hens equally with the rice mixture. Place the stuffed hens in a large baking pan coated with nonstick cooking spray. In a medium saucepan, combine the chicken broth, orange juice, honey, and cornstarch. Cook over medium heat, stirring constantly, until thickened and bubbly, about 3 to 5 minutes. Pour the sauce over the hens. Bake for 1 hour, or until the meat is tender, basting every 20 minutes. If the hens brown too quickly, cover with foil. Remove skin and cut in half to serve.

Makes 12 servings

Nutritional information per serving

Calories	455	Cal. from Fat (%)	26.9	Sodium (g)	300
Fat (g)	13.6	Saturated Fat (g)	3.8	Cholesterol (mg)	160
Protein (g)	54	Carbohydrate (g)	26		

75

Chicken, Broccoli, and Rice

This is one of those last-minute dinners that feed the family and make you look good in the kitchen.

1 tablespoon light stick
  margarine
1¼ cups rice
2 cups wide noodles
1½ pounds skinless, boneless
  chicken breasts, cut into
  1½-inch pieces
2 (14½-ounce) cans fat-free
  chicken broth

4 cups broccoli florets
1 cup chopped tomato
1 teaspoon dried basil
Salt and pepper to taste
1 cup shredded part-skim
  mozzarella cheese

In a large, deep skillet coated with nonstick cooking spray, melt the margarine and brown the rice over medium-high heat for 3 to 4 minutes, stirring constantly. Add the noodles, chicken, and chicken broth and bring to a boil over high heat. Spread the broccoli over the top, reduce the heat, cover, and cook for 10 minutes. Add the tomato and gently stir, mixing thoroughly. Cover and continue cooking over a low heat for 10 minutes longer, or until most of the liquid is absorbed and the rice and noodles are done. Season with basil and salt and pepper, mixing carefully. Sprinkle with the mozzarella, cover, and cook for 1 to 2 minutes longer, or until the cheese melts.

Makes 6 servings

Nutritional information per serving

Calories	563	Cal. from Fat (%)	14	Sodium (g)	349
Fat (g)	8.8	Saturated Fat (g)	3.2	Cholesterol (mg)	80
Protein (g)	42	Carbohydrate (g)	76.4		

Glazed Turkey
with Cornbread Stuffing

The cornbread stuffing complements the turkey and makes this a wonderful meal. It's like celebrating Thanksgiving any time of the year.

1 onion, chopped	1 teaspoon dried thyme
½ cup chopped celery	1 cup apricot-pineapple
3 cups spinach, washed,	preserves
torn, and stemmed	1 tablespoon Dijon mustard
1½ cups packaged	2 tablespoons packaged dry
cornbread stuffing	onion soup and recipe mix
½ cup fat-free canned	3 pounds skinless, boneless
chicken broth	turkey breasts
1 large egg white	Salt and pepper to taste

Preheat the oven to 350° F. In a large skillet coated with nonstick cooking spray, sauté the onion and celery over medium heat until tender, about 5 to 7 minutes. Stir in the spinach and sauté just until the spinach is wilted, about 5 minutes. Remove from the heat and add the cornbread stuffing, chicken broth, egg white, and thyme, stirring until well combined. Place the stuffing in a 2-quart oblong baking dish coated with nonstick cooking spray. In a small bowl, mix together the preserves, mustard, and onion soup mix. Lay the turkey on top of the stuffing and season. Pour the sauce over the top. Bake, uncovered, for 1 hour, or until the turkey is done. Baste with the sauce during cooking, and cover loosely with foil during cooking if the turkey browns too quickly.

Makes 6 servings

Nutritional information per serving

Calories	540	Cal. from Fat (%)	5.7	Sodium (g)	1,065
Fat (g)	3.4	Saturated Fat (g)	0.9	Cholesterol (mg)	149
Protein (g)	59.9	Carbohydrate (g)	66.7		

Turkey and Rice Bake

The maple syrup gives this turkey dish a New England feel and makes a nice change of pace.

1⅓ cups rice	2 pounds skinless, boneless
1 (14½-ounce) can fat-free	turkey breasts
chicken broth	Salt and pepper to taste
1 (10½-ounce) can French	⅓ cup maple syrup
onion soup	

Preheat oven to 350° F. In a 2-quart oblong baking dish, mix the rice, chicken broth, and onion soup, stirring well. Lay the turkey breasts along the top of the rice. Season with salt and pepper. Drizzle the maple syrup over the top. Cover tightly with foil and bake for 1 hour and 15 minutes, or until all the liquid is absorbed and the turkey is tender.

Makes 6 servings

Nutritional information per serving

Calories	402	Cal. from Fat (%)	4.4	Sodium (g)	668
Fat (g)	2	Saturated Fat (g)	0.5	Cholesterol (mg)	99
Protein (g)	41.4	Carbohydrate (g)	52.4		

MEATS

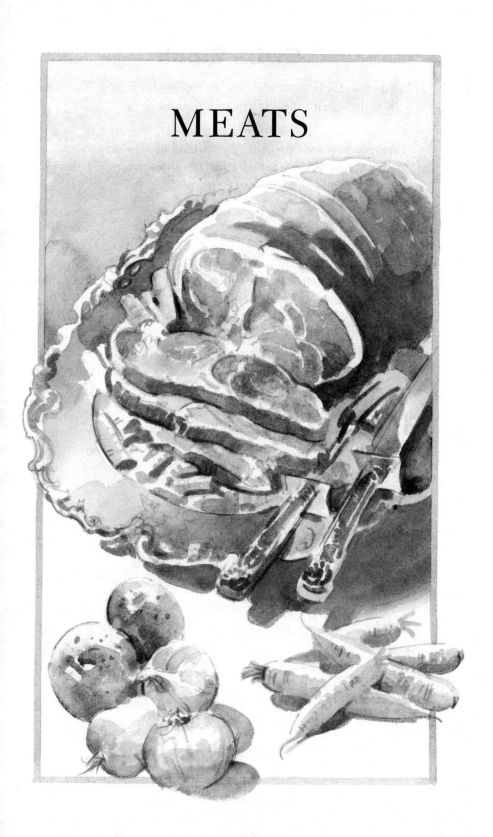

Swiss Steak

I like to serve Swiss steak with wild rice mixed with peas. The colors as well as the flavors make it a winning combination.

1½ cups chopped onion
1 teaspoon minced garlic
½ pound mushrooms, sliced
2 pounds round steak
Salt and pepper to taste
1 (14½-ounce) can no-salt-
   added whole tomatoes,
   chopped, with their juices

1 (8-ounce) can no-salt-
   added tomato sauce
1 (16-ounce) package baby
   carrots

In a large skillet coated with nonstick cooking spray, sauté the onion, garlic, and mushrooms over medium heat until tender, about 5 minutes. Trim any fat from the round steak and season with salt and pepper. Add the meat to the skillet and brown on both sides for about 7 minutes. Add the tomatoes, tomato sauce, and carrots. Bring to a boil, reduce the heat, and cook, covered, until the meat is very tender, about 1½ to 2 hours.

Makes 6 servings

Nutritional information per serving

Calories	259	Cal. from Fat (%)	21.7	Sodium (g)	80
Fat (g)	6.2	Saturated Fat (g)	2.1	Cholesterol (mg)	80
Protein (g)	34.7	Carbohydrate (g)	15.4		

Chicken and Beef Shish Kabobs

Marinating the chicken and beef in the orange and wine marinade overnight makes this dish extra-special. The marinade is good with other meats and poultry as well. You can skewer all-chicken and all-meat shish kabobs or make each skewer a combination. It's worth firing up that grill hot for this recipe. Of course, the shish kabobs can be broiled indoors also.

2 pounds boneless, skinless
   chicken breasts, cut into
   1½-inch cubes
2 pounds sirloin tip, cut into
   1½ cubes
1 pint cherry tomatoes

1 pound mushrooms
2 green bell peppers, seeded
   and cut into chunks
1 onion, cut into chunks
Orange and Wine Marinade
   (recipe follows)

Place the chicken, meat, tomatoes, mushrooms, peppers, and onion in a large bowl and pour the Orange and Wine Marinade over them. Refrigerate overnight. Assemble the meat and vegetables on metal skewers, without crowding the pieces together, and grill on a hot grill 5 to 10 minutes, turning frequently. Baste with the remaining marinade while grilling.

Makes 8 to 10 skewers

Orange and Wine Marinade

1 cup dry red wine
¼ cup reduced-sodium soy
   sauce
1 cup orange juice
1 tablespoon dried thyme

1 tablespoon dried rosemary
2 tablespoons
   Worcestershire sauce
1 tablespoon pepper
1 tablespoon minced garlic

Mix together the wine, soy sauce, orange juice, thyme, rosemary, Worcestershire sauce, pepper, and garlic in a bowl.

Nutritional information per serving

Calories	292	Cal. from Fat (%)	27	Sodium (g)	272
Fat (g)	8.8	Saturated Fat (g)	3.1	Cholesterol (mg)	107
Protein (g)	39.4	Carbohydrate (g)	9.9		

Italian Eggplant, Meat, and Rice ♥

This hearty dish topped with tomato sauce and cheese will be very popular. Even if you're not an eggplant fan, this dish will win you over. It's kind of like a rice dressing—most people don't even realize it has eggplant. Great to feed a crowd!

2 medium eggplants, peeled
  and cubed
1 zucchini, thinly sliced
1 tablespoon minced garlic
4 ounces light bulk sausage
½ pound ground sirloin
Salt and pepper to taste
1 tablespoon plus 1 teaspoon
  dried basil, divided

1 tablespoon plus 1 teaspoon
  dried oregano, divided
3 cups cooked rice
1 (15-ounce) can no-salt-
  added tomato sauce
1¾ cups shredded part-skim
  mozzarella cheese

Preheat the oven to 350° F. In a large pot coated with nonstick cooking spray, sauté the eggplant, zucchini, garlic, sausage, and meat over medium heat until the meat is done and the vegetables are very tender, about 10 minutes. Drain any excess grease. Add the salt and pepper, 1 tablespoon of the basil, 1 tablespoon of the oregano, and the cooked rice, tossing well. Spread the mixture in a 2-quart casserole dish coated with nonstick cooking spray. Combine the tomato sauce with the remaining basil and oregano and spread over the eggplant-rice mixture. Sprinkle with the mozzarella and bake, uncovered, for 20 to 30 minutes, or until the mixture is hot and the cheese is melted.

Makes 6 to 8 servings

Nutritional information per serving

Calories	269	Cal. from Fat (%)	29.9	Sodium (g)	296
Fat (g)	8.9	Saturated Fat (g)	4.3	Cholesterol (mg)	43
Protein (g)	18.4	Carbohydrate (g)	29.1		

Sloppy Joes

With the addition of corn and carrots, this oldie becomes a goodie—
and the kids still love it.

½ cup chopped onion
½ cup shredded peeled
  carrots
1 pound ground sirloin
2 (8-ounce) cans no-salt-
  added tomato sauce

⅓ cup barbecue sauce
1 (11-ounce) can Mexicorn,
  drained
1 tablespoon light brown
  sugar
4 bun halves, toasted

In a large skillet coated with nonstick cooking spray, cook the onion,
carrots, and meat over medium heat until done, about 10 minutes.
Drain off any excess grease. Add the tomato sauce, barbecue sauce,
corn, and brown sugar, cooking for 5 minutes until well heated.
Spoon onto the bun halves.

Makes 4 servings

Nutritional information per serving

Calories	415	Cal. from Fat (%)	23.1	Sodium (g)	756
Fat (g)	10.7	Saturated Fat (g)	3.7	Cholesterol (mg)	68
Protein (g)	30.5	Carbohydrate (g)	50.4		

Hearty Hamburger Meal

This is just as easy as a certain packaged mix, but you know exactly what's in it. If you have an adventurous family, add some black olives.

1 pound ground sirloin	1 tablespoon Worcestershire
1 cup chopped onion	sauce
1 teaspoon minced garlic	1 bay leaf
1 (10½-ounce) can beef	1 (8-ounce) package small
broth	shell pasta
2 (8-ounce) cans no-salt-	1 (15¼-ounce) can whole-
added tomato sauce	kernel corn, drained

In a large skillet coated with nonstick cooking spray, cook the meat, onion, and garlic over medium heat, about 5 minutes. Add the beef broth, tomato sauce, Worcestershire sauce, and bay leaf and stir well. Bring to a boil and simmer for 10 minutes. Add the pasta, reduce the heat, and simmer, covered, stirring occasionally for 20 minutes, or until the pasta is done. Add the corn and heat thoroughly. Discard the bay leaf.

Makes 4 servings

Nutritional information per serving

Calories	514	Cal. from Fat (%) 17.2		Sodium (g)	536
Fat (g)	9.8	Saturated Fat (g) 3.4		Cholesterol (mg)	68
Protein (g)	35.4	Carbohydrate (g) 72.4			

Barbecue Burger and Bean Bake ♥

When the weather isn't cooperating, bring the fantastic taste of barbecue inside. If you want to make this a vegetarian dish, leave out the sirloin and serve over rice.

1 pound ground sirloin
1 onion, chopped
1 tablespoon Worcestershire sauce
½ teaspoon pepper
½ teaspoon chili powder
1 tablespoon prepared mustard
¼ cup ketchup
1 (8-ounce) can no-salt-added tomato sauce

⅓ cup light brown sugar
½ cup water
2 (15-ounce) cans pinto beans, drained and rinsed
1 (15½-ounce) can lima beans, drained and rinsed
1 (15-ounce) can red kidney beans, drained and rinsed
1 (15½-ounce) can Great Northern beans, drained and rinsed

In a large skillet coated with nonstick cooking spray, cook the meat and onion over medium heat until the meat is done, about 5 to 7 minutes. Drain any excess grease. Preheat the oven to 350° F. In a 3-quart casserole dish coated with nonstick cooking spray, combine the meat mixture with the Worcestershire sauce, pepper, chili powder, mustard, ketchup, tomato sauce, brown sugar, water, pinto beans, lima beans, kidney beans, and Great Northern beans, mixing well. Bake, covered, for 1 hour.

Makes 4 to 6 servings

Nutritional information per serving

Calories	343	Cal. from Fat (%)	16.4	Sodium (g)	860
Fat (g)	6.3	Saturated Fat (g)	2.2	Cholesterol (mg)	45
Protein (g)	27.7	Carbohydrate (g)	47.3		

Sirloin Strips with Dijon Mushroom Sauce

The rich sauce with its slight Dijon flavor will delight your family. You'll be happy, too—especially since you don't have to do much more than open up a can of mushroom soup!

1½ pounds boneless sirloin
  steak, ¾ inch thick,
  trimmed of fat, and cut
  into strips
½ pound mushrooms, sliced
1 cup sliced onion
1 teaspoon minced garlic

1 (10¾-ounce) can reduced-fat
  cream of mushroom soup
2 tablespoons Dijon mustard
1 tablespoon Worcestershire
  sauce
¼ teaspoon pepper
4 cups cooked rice

In a large skillet coated with nonstick cooking spray, cook the meat until brown, about 5 minutes. Drain any excess fat from the pan. Coat the pan again with cooking spray and add the mushrooms, onion, and garlic. Sauté until the vegetables are tender and the meat is done, about 5 minutes. Add the cream of mushroom soup, mustard, Worcestershire sauce, and pepper. Bring to a boil, lower the heat, and cook another 5 minutes. Serve over the rice.

Makes 4 to 6 servings

Nutritional information per serving

Calories	356	Cal. from Fat (%)	23.7	Sodium (g)	343
Fat (g)	9.4	Saturated Fat (g)	3.5	Cholesterol (mg)	72
Protein (g)	27	Carbohydrate (g)	38.9		

Spinach Beef Casserole

This casserole turned out to be an unexpected favorite—especially of mine, because it can be made ahead and cooked later, or frozen after cooking and reheated in a 300° F oven.

1¼ pounds ground sirloin
1 medium onion, chopped
1 (8-ounce) can mushroom
  stems and pieces, drained
1 tablespoon minced garlic
1 teaspoon dried oregano
2 (10-ounce) packages
  frozen chopped spinach,
  thawed and squeezed dry

1 (10¾-ounce) can reduced-
  fat cream of celery soup
½ cup rice
½ cup skim milk
Salt and pepper to taste
1 cup shredded reduced-fat
  mozzarella cheese

Preheat the oven to 350° F. In a large skillet, cook the meat, onion, mushrooms, garlic, and oregano over medium-high heat until the meat is done, about 5 to 8 minutes. Drain any excess grease. Spoon into a 2-quart casserole dish coated with nonstick cooking spray. Mix in the spinach, cream of celery soup, rice, milk, and salt and pepper. Transfer to a 2-quart casserole dish coated with nonstick cooking spray. Bake for 35 to 45 minutes. Sprinkle the mozzarella on top and continue baking 5 minutes more, or until the cheese is melted.

Makes 6 servings

Nutritional information per serving

Calories	316	Cal. from Fat (%)	30.1	Sodium (g)	685
Fat (g)	10.6	Saturated Fat (g)	4.9	Cholesterol (mg)	66
Protein (g)	29.7	Carbohydrate (g)	25.5		

Mock Cabbage Rolls

This recipe is a quick-and-easy alternative to individually stuffing all those cabbage leaves.

1½ pounds ground sirloin
1 onion, chopped
1 teaspoon minced garlic
¼ teaspoon pepper
3 cups cooked rice
1 (¾ pound) head of cabbage, coarsely shredded

1 (27-ounce) jar spaghetti sauce
¼ cup light brown sugar
1 cup shredded part-skim mozzarella cheese

Preheat the oven to 350° F. In a large skillet, cook the meat, onion, and garlic until the meat is done, about 8 minutes. Drain any excess grease. Add the pepper and the cooked rice, mixing well. Spoon the meat mixture into a 4-quart casserole dish coated with nonstick cooking spray. Top with the shredded cabbage. In a bowl, mix together the spaghetti sauce and brown sugar. Pour the sauce over the cabbage. Bake, covered, for 1 hour and 15 minutes, or until the cabbage is tender. Sprinkle with the mozzarella and continue baking for 5 minutes, or until the cheese is melted.

Makes 6 to 8 servings

Nutritional information per serving

Calories	384	Cal. from Fat (%)	30.4	Sodium (g)	596
Fat (g)	13	Saturated Fat (g)	4.5	Cholesterol (mg)	59
Protein (g)	24.7	Carbohydrate (g)	42.3		

Roasted Eye of Round and Vegetables

This roast, marinated overnight in red wine and onion soup, can also be sliced thinly and used for sandwiches.

1 (3-pound) eye of round roast
1 tablespoon minced garlic
½ teaspoon pepper
1 teaspoon dried thyme
1 cup dry red wine
1 (10½-ounce) can French onion soup

1 bay leaf, crumbled
1 (1-pound) package carrots, peeled and cut into 3-inch chunks
1 onion, quartered
3 red potatoes, peeled and cut into quarters

Make slits in the roast and stuff with the garlic. Rub the meat with the pepper and thyme. Place the meat in a shallow roasting pan. In a small bowl, combine the wine, onion soup, and bay leaf. Pour over the meat. Cover well with plastic wrap and refrigerate overnight, or at least several hours, turning occasionally. Preheat the oven to 450° F. Place the roast in a shallow open roasting pan, reserving the marinade. Arrange the carrots, onion, and potatoes around the meat. Roast for 20 minutes. Pour the reserved marinade over the roast and continue cooking for 25 minutes longer, or until the vegetables are tender and the meat is done. Slice the meat diagonally across the grain into thin slices and serve with the vegetables.

Makes 6 to 8 servings

Nutritional information per serving

Calories	296	Cal. from Fat (%)	22	Sodium (g)	361
Fat (g)	7.2	Saturated Fat (g)	2.6	Cholesterol (mg)	86
Protein (g)	38.3	Carbohydrate (g)	14.3		

Spicy Citrus Beef

With this dish, you hit several food groups. The light orange sauce with spicy high notes of ginger and red pepper brings out the best of the beef.

⅓ cup thawed frozen orange
   juice concentrate
¼ cup reduced-sodium soy
   sauce
¼ cup dry white wine
2 tablespoons cornstarch
1 teaspoon grated orange
   rind
1 teaspoon sugar
1 tablespoon minced garlic
6 cups broccoli florets

1 teaspoon ground ginger
½ teaspoon crushed red
   pepper flakes
1½ pounds boneless beef
   sirloin, cut into thin 2-inch
   strips
3 medium seedless oranges,
   peeled and sectioned
   (about 3 cups)
1 bunch green onions
   (scallions), sliced

In a small bowl, combine the orange juice, soy sauce, wine, cornstarch, orange rind, and sugar; set aside. In a large skillet or wok coated with nonstick cooking spray, sauté the garlic, broccoli, ginger, and red pepper over medium-high heat for 2 minutes, stirring. Add the meat and continue to sauté, stirring constantly, until the meat is browned. Add the orange juice mixture and continue cooking, stirring constantly, until slightly thickened, about 2 minutes. Add the orange sections and green onions, and cook until heated, about 2 minutes.

Makes 4 to 6 servings

Nutritional information per serving

Calories	278	Cal. from Fat (%) 26.3	Sodium (g)	400
Fat (g)	8.1	Saturated Fat (g) 3.1	Cholesterol (mg)	68
Protein (g)	27	Carbohydrate (g) 24.4		

Beefy Jamaican Stir-Fry

If you like very spicy dishes, give this very unusual but addictive dish a try!

1 pound lean flank steak	1 green bell pepper, seeded
¼ cup rum	and cut into julienne strips
1 tablespoon Dijon mustard	½ cup sliced green onions
1 teaspoon cornstarch	(scallions)
1 teaspoon minced garlic	1 cup shredded peeled
1 teaspoon dried thyme	carrots
¼ teaspoon cayenne pepper	1 cup coarsely chopped
¼ teaspoon ground allspice	tomato
Dash of ground cinnamon	1 cup chopped zucchini
Dash of ground nutmeg	4 cups cooked rice
1 teaspoon sugar	

Trim any fat from the flank steak. Slice the steak diagonally across the grain into ¼-inch-wide strips. Combine the rum, mustard, cornstarch, garlic, thyme, cayenne, allspice, cinnamon, nutmeg, and sugar in a small bowl; stir well and set aside. Coat a large skillet with nonstick cooking spray and heat over medium-high heat. Add the steak and stir-fry for 5 minutes, or until browned. Remove from the skillet; set aside. Again coat the skillet with nonstick cooking spray and add the green pepper, green onions, carrots, tomato, and zucchini; sauté over medium-high heat for 3 minutes. Return the steak and the rum mixture to the pan. Stir-fry for 1 to 2 minutes, or until the mixture is slightly thickened. Serve the steak over the rice.

Makes 4 servings

Nutritional information per serving

Calories	457	Cal. from Fat (%) 23.1	Sodium (g)	714
Fat (g)	11.7	Saturated Fat (g) 4.7	Cholesterol (mg)	47
Protein (g)	23.6	Carbohydrate (g) 54.9		

Smoked Pork Scallopini Dinner

This dish will appeal to those who like sauerkraut. It has a slightly sweet, smoky flavor, and the caraway seeds give it a distinct personality.

2 pounds pork scallopini
  (thin slices)
1 tablespoon liquid smoke
1 medium tart baking apple,
  peeled and cored
2 cups sliced peeled carrots

2 (14-ounce) cans
  sauerkraut, drained
1 (12-ounce) can light beer
⅓ cup light brown sugar
2 teaspoons caraway seeds
½ cup water

Trim any excess fat from the pork. In a large skillet coated with non-stick cooking spray, cook the pork with the liquid smoke over high heat until browned, in batches if necessary, about 5 minutes for each batch. Meanwhile, coarsely grate half of the apple, reserving the remaining half. With all the pork in the skillet, add the carrots, grated apple, sauerkraut, beer, brown sugar, caraway seeds, and water. Heat to boiling over high heat. Reduce the heat to low, cover, and simmer 35 minutes. Grate the remaining apple and add to the mixture in the skillet. Cook for 10 minutes longer, or until the carrots and pork are fork-tender, occasionally spooning the liquid in the skillet over the pork.

Makes 4 servings

Nutritional information per serving

Calories	482	Cal. from Fat (%)	20.5	Sodium (g)	1,470
Fat (g)	11	Saturated Fat (g)	3.8	Cholesterol (mg)	134
Protein (g)	50.4	Carbohydrate (g)	40.9		

Old-Fashioned Pork Chop Casserole

In this easy standby, you get gravy, meat, and rice, in a no-fail combination, which appeals to everyone in my house.

⅔ cup rice
1 (6-ounce) package long-grain and wild rice
3 cups hot water
8 bone-in loin pork chops, trimmed of all fat (½ inch thick)

¼ teaspoon pepper
1 (10¾-ounce) can reduced-fat cream of celery soup
⅔ cup skim milk
⅓ cup chopped green onions (scallions)

Preheat the oven to 350° F. Combine the rice, wild rice with its seasoning packet, and hot water. Place the rice mixture in a 13 × 9 × 2-inch baking dish coated with nonstick cooking spray; lay the pork chops on top and sprinkle with the pepper. Cover and bake for 1 hour. Mix together the cream of celery soup, milk, and green onions. Uncover the casserole and pour the soup mixture over the pork chops. Return the casserole, uncovered, to the oven and bake for 15 minutes longer, or until thoroughly heated.

Makes 6 to 8 servings

Nutritional information per serving

Calories	323	Cal. from Fat (%)	22	Sodium (g)	591
Fat (g)	7.9	Saturated Fat (g)	2.7	Cholesterol (mg)	69
Protein (g)	27.6	Carbohydrate (g)	34		

Pork Chop and Lima Bean Skillet Supper

The brown sugar gives the sauce a slightly sweet flavor that goes especially well with the pork. Serve it over rice to sop up all the wonderful sauce.

6 thick, center-cut boneless
pork chops
1 onion, finely chopped
4 medium carrots, peeled
and thinly sliced
1 teaspoon minced garlic
1 (28-ounce) can no-salt-
added whole tomatoes,
crushed, with their juices

2 tablespoons light brown
sugar
⅛ teaspoon pepper
1 (16-ounce) package frozen
baby lima beans, partially
thawed

In a large skillet coated with nonstick cooking spray, brown the pork chops on each side, 5 minutes per side, cooking them in batches if necessary. Remove to a platter. Add the onion to the skillet and cook, stirring occasionally, until soft, about 5 minutes. Stir in the carrots and garlic and sauté 5 minutes more. Add the tomatoes, sugar, and pepper. Return the pork chops to the skillet. Bring to a boil, reduce the heat to low, cover, and simmer for 20 minutes. Stir in the lima beans, pushing them down into the liquid. Simmer, uncovered, until the pork chops are tender and no longer pink on the inside, about 25 minutes longer.

Makes 6 servings

Nutritional information per serving

Calories	306	Cal. from Fat (%)	19.8	Sodium (g)	94
Fat (g)	6.7	Saturated Fat (g)	2.2	Cholesterol (mg)	67
Protein (g)	29.8	Carbohydrate (g)	31.1		

Pork and Wild Rice Stir-Fry

By slicing the pork tenderloin in thin slices and combining it with the wild rice, you get a very delicious and nutritious dish. Since the rice is mixed with all the other ingredients, the flavors blend together wonderfully.

1 (6-ounce) package long-grain and wild rice
1 pound pork tenderloin, sliced ⅛ inch thick
1 cup diagonally sliced celery
1 cup green bell pepper, seeded and cut into strips
1 bunch green onions (scallions), sliced
½ pound mushrooms, sliced
1 (8-ounce) can sliced water chestnuts, drained
2 teaspoons ground ginger
1 (6-ounce) package frozen pea pods, thawed
1½ tablespoons cornstarch
¼ cup reduced-sodium soy sauce
2 tablespoons dry sherry

Cook the wild rice according to package directions, omitting any oil and salt; set aside. Meanwhile, in a large, heavy skillet coated with nonstick cooking spray, stir-fry the pork over medium-high heat for 2 minutes, or until the meat is no longer pink. Add the celery, green pepper, green onions, mushrooms, water chestnuts, and ginger. Stir-fry 5 minutes, or until the vegetables are crisp-tender. Stir in the wild rice and pea pods; move the mixture up the side of the skillet, letting the juices cover the bottom of the pan. Mix the cornstarch, soy sauce, and sherry in a small bowl. Add to the juices in the pan; cook about 1 minute, or until thickened. Toss the vegetables and pork with the sauce gently to coat.

Makes 4 to 6 servings

Nutritional information per serving

Calories	278	Cal. from Fat (%)	13.3	Sodium (g)	696
Fat (g)	4.1	Saturated Fat (g)	1.3	Cholesterol (mg)	45
Protein (g)	22.1	Carbohydrate (g)	37.3		

Pork Tenderloin Diane

While the rice is cooking, you can prepare this quick, fancy-tasting pork dish.

1 (6-ounce) package long-
  grain and wild rice
2 pounds pork tenderloin,
  cut crosswise into 16 slices,
  each about 1 inch thick
2 teaspoons pepper
2 tablespoons light stick
  margarine

¼ cup lemon juice
2 tablespoons
  Worcestershire sauce
1 tablespoon Dijon mustard
1 tablespoon chopped
  parsley

Cook the wild rice according to package directions, omitting any oil and salt. Meanwhile, sprinkle the pork slices with pepper. Heat the margarine in a heavy skillet. Cook the slices 3 to 4 minutes on each side until browned, working in batches if necessary. Remove to a serving platter and cover to keep warm. Add the lemon juice, Worcestershire sauce, and mustard to the skillet. Cook, stirring with the pork juices, until heated thoroughly. Return the pork to the sauce. Serve the pork and sauce over the rice and sprinkle with the parsley.

Makes 4 servings

Nutritional information per serving

Calories	487	Cal. from Fat (%)	27.5	Sodium (g)	746
Fat (g)	14.9	Saturated Fat (g)	4.4	Cholesterol (mg)	134
Protein (g)	52.2	Carbohydrate (g)	34.3		

Italian Pork, Squash, and Tomatoes

All the fresh vegetables cooked together form a wonderful sauce full of flavor. I enjoy this dish especially in the summer, when the squash is at its best.

2 pounds pork tenderloin, trimmed and cut into 1½-inch cubes
2 cups sliced yellow squash (about 3 squash)
1 large zucchini, sliced
1 green bell pepper, seeded and coarsely chopped
1 onion, coarsely chopped
1 teaspoon minced garlic
4 large Roma (plum) tomatoes, quartered
1 teaspoon dried basil
1 teaspoon dried oregano
1 (28-ounce) can no-salt-added whole tomatoes, crushed, with their juices
6 cups cooked rice

Heat a large skillet coated with nonstick cooking spray over high heat and add the pork, squash, zucchini, green pepper, onion, garlic, tomatoes, basil, and oregano. Cook, stirring, until the meat begins to brown and the vegetables are crisp-tender, about 10 minutes. Add the crushed tomatoes and continue cooking, covered, over medium heat until the meat is done and the vegetables are tender, about 20 minutes. Serve over the rice.

Makes 6 servings

Nutritional information per serving

Calories	462	Cal. from Fat (%)	15.2	Sodium (g)	83
Fat (g)	7.8	Saturated Fat (g)	2.6	Cholesterol (mg)	90
Protein (g)	38.5	Carbohydrate (g)	57.4		

Veal and Tomatoes with Angel Hair ♥

Veal and pasta can be combined in many different ways, but here the spices, olives, and prosciutto give this dish a unique personality. There is not a lot of sauce in this dish, but there is a lot of flavor.

1 (12-ounce) package angel hair (capellini) pasta
1 large onion, thinly sliced
½ pound veal scaloppini, cut into 1-inch strips
2 tablespoons all-purpose flour
½ cup dry white wine
1 teaspoon minced garlic
Salt and pepper to taste

1 teaspoon dried oregano
1 teaspoon dried thyme
5 Roma (plum) tomatoes, cut into wedges
1 (2¼-ounce) can sliced ripe black olives, drained
2 ounces prosciutto, cut into 1-inch strips
2 tablespoons chopped parsley

Cook the pasta according to package directions, omitting any oil and salt; drain and set aside. Meanwhile, in a large skillet coated with nonstick cooking spray, sauté the onion over medium heat until tender, about 5 minutes. Sprinkle the veal with the flour and add the veal to the skillet, stirring constantly, cooking the veal until lightly browned. Stir in the wine, garlic, salt and pepper, oregano, and thyme. Bring to a boil, cover, reduce the heat, and simmer 8 to 10 minutes, or until the veal is almost tender. Add the tomatoes and olives, cover, and simmer 5 minutes, or until thoroughly heated. Place the prosciutto on top of the veal, cover, and let stand 2 minutes. Serve the veal mixture over the pasta, sprinkled with parsley.

Makes 4 to 6 servings

Nutritional information per serving

Calories	343	Cal. from Fat (%)	11.9	Sodium (g)	208
Fat (g)	4.5	Saturated Fat (g)	1.2	Cholesterol (mg)	24
Protein (g)	16.4	Carbohydrate (g)	55.7		

SEAFOOD

Shrimp and Rice Florentine

The green spinach blended with the yellow and white rice makes this dish attractive and a great-tasting casserole. Prepare ahead of time; it freezes really well.

1 (5-ounce) package yellow saffron rice
1 cup chopped onion
1 teaspoon minced garlic
1½ pounds medium shrimp, peeled
1 (10¾-ounce) can reduced-fat cream of mushroom soup
1 cup shredded reduced-fat Monterey Jack cheese

⅓ cup dry sherry
2 cups cooked rice
1 (8-ounce) can sliced water chestnuts, drained
2 (10-ounce) packages frozen chopped spinach, cooked and drained
¼ cup grated Parmesan cheese, divided
Salt and pepper to taste

Preheat the oven to 350° F. Cook the saffron rice according to package directions, omitting any oil and salt. In a large skillet coated with nonstick cooking spray, sauté the onion and garlic until the onion is tender, about 5 minutes. Add the shrimp and cook until the shrimp turn pink, about 5 minutes. Stir in the mushroom soup, Monterey Jack, and sherry, heating until the soup is warm. Add the saffron rice, rice, water chestnuts, and spinach, 2 tablespoons of the Parmesan, and salt and pepper. Pour into a 2-quart casserole coated with nonstick cooking spray. Sprinkle with the remaining Parmesan. Bake, uncovered, 25 to 30 minutes, or until bubbly.

Makes 8 servings

Nutritional information per serving

Calories	304	Cal. from Fat (%)	16.4	Sodium (g)	814
Fat (g)	5.5	Saturated Fat (g)	3.1	Cholesterol (mg)	136
Protein (g)	22.5	Carbohydrate (g)	38.5		

Herbed Shrimp and Pasta Casserole

When you add eggs to the pasta, it forms a distinct custardy layer. This unique casserole is great for a light evening meal.

1 (8-ounce) package angel hair (capellini) pasta
1 large egg white
1 large egg
1 cup evaporated skimmed milk
1 cup plain nonfat yogurt
¼ cup chopped parsley
1 teaspoon dried basil
1 teaspoon dried oregano
1 teaspoon minced garlic
1 (16-ounce) jar mild chunky salsa
½ pound medium shrimp, peeled
1½ cups shredded part-skim mozzarella cheese

Preheat the oven to 350° F. Cook the pasta according to package directions, omitting any oil and salt. Drain and set aside. In a bowl, blend together the egg white, egg, evaporated milk, yogurt, parsley, basil, oregano, and garlic; set aside. Spread half of the pasta over the bottom of a 13 × 9 × 2-inch baking dish coated with nonstick cooking spray. Cover with the salsa. Layer half of the shrimp over the salsa. Spread the remaining pasta over the shrimp. Pour the egg mixture evenly over the pasta. Cover with the remaining shrimp and top with the mozzarella. Bake, uncovered, 30 minutes, or until the shrimp are done and the liquid is absorbed. Remove from the oven and let stand 10 minutes before serving.

Makes 6 servings

Nutritional information per serving

Calories	346	Cal. from Fat (%)	17.1	Sodium (g)	817
Fat (g)	6.6	Saturated Fat (g)	3.4	Cholesterol (mg)	108
Protein (g)	24.9	Carbohydrate (g)	44.3		

Tropical Shrimp Salsa over Rice

Tropical, spicy flavors lend a Polynesian air to this dish. The fruit provides a sweetness, while the salsa gives it bite. Choose the piquancy of the salsa according to how hot you like your food.

2 pounds medium shrimp, peeled
Salt and pepper to taste
1 (28-ounce) can no-salt-added diced tomatoes, drained
1 cup thick and chunky salsa

1 (8-ounce) can crushed pineapple, with their juices
$\frac{1}{2}$ cup orange juice
$\frac{1}{4}$ cup chopped parsley
4 cups cooked rice

In a skillet coated with nonstick cooking spray, sauté the shrimp over medium heat until pink, about 5 minutes. Season with salt and pepper. Add the tomatoes, salsa, pineapple, orange juice, and parsley. Cook for 10 minutes, until well blended and hot. Serve over the cooked rice.

Makes 4 to 6 servings

Nutritional information per serving

Calories	311	Cal. from Fat (%)	4.6	Sodium (g)	537
Fat (g)	1.6	Saturated Fat (g)	0.4	Cholesterol (mg)	215
Protein (g)	27.3	Carbohydrate (g)	44.2		

Shrimp with Dill

Dill enhances the flavor of this simple dish. For a treat, you can use large shrimp, but medium ones will work fine, too.

3 tablespoons light stick margarine, melted
1 bunch green onions (scallions), chopped
1 tablespoon minced garlic
2 pounds large shrimp, peeled and deveined

$\frac{1}{4}$ cup dry white wine
$\frac{1}{8}$ cup lemon juice
Salt and pepper to taste
$1\frac{1}{2}$ teaspoons dried dillweed
1 tablespoon chopped parsley
3 cups cooked rice

In a large skillet, melt the margarine over medium heat and cook the green onions and garlic, stirring constantly, 2 minutes. Add the shrimp, wine, lemon juice, and salt and pepper; cook over medium heat until the shrimp turn pink, about 5 to 8 minutes, stirring occasionally. Stir in the dillweed and parsley. Serve immediately over the rice.

Makes 4 servings

Nutritional information per serving

Calories	399	Cal. from Fat (%) 18.6	Sodium (g)	472
Fat (g)	8.2	Saturated Fat (g) 1.7	Cholesterol (mg)	323
Protein (g)	38.8	Carbohydrate (g) 37.7		

Stir-Fried Shrimp and Scallops

This is a classic seafood stir-fry that no one will be able to resist. I prefer sea scallops, halved, but either type of scallop will work.

2 cups rice

2 tablespoons reduced-sodium soy sauce

2 tablespoons rice vinegar

1 red or yellow bell pepper, seeded and cut into $\frac{1}{2}$-inch squares

1 large carrot, peeled and coarsely shredded

1 (8-ounce) can sliced water chestnuts, drained

1 (6-ounce) package frozen pea pods

$1\frac{1}{2}$ teaspoons sugar

1 pound medium shrimp, peeled

1 pound bay scallops or halved sea scallops

1 bunch green onions (scallions), chopped

$\frac{1}{2}$ teaspoon ground ginger

Cook the rice according to package directions, omitting any oil and salt; set aside. Meanwhile, combine the soy sauce and vinegar in a small bowl and set aside. In a large skillet coated with nonstick cooking spray over medium-high heat, combine the bell pepper, carrot, water chestnuts, and pea pods, sprinkle with the sugar, and stir until glossy, about 3 to 5 minutes. Add the shrimp and scallops and stir-fry for 5 minutes. Add the green onions and ginger and stir-fry for 1 minute longer. Add the soy mixture and cook, uncovered, stirring occasionally, about 1 minute, or until the mixture is syrupy and the shrimp and scallops are cooked through. Serve over the rice.

Makes 6 servings

Nutritional information per serving

Calories	435	Cal. from Fat (%) 4.1	Sodium (g)	461
Fat (g)	2	Saturated Fat (g) 0.4	Cholesterol (mg)	133
Protein (g)	31.7	Carbohydrate (g) 70		

Shrimp Stuffed Peppers

The shrimp rice mixture is flavored with tomato and makes a wonderful filling for the peppers. Choose an assortment of colored peppers for the prettiest presentation. If you don't feel like messing with the peppers, the mixture can be baked as a casserole also.

1 onion, chopped
1 teaspoon minced garlic
1 (8-ounce) can no-salt-added tomato sauce
1 (14½-ounce) can no-salt-added diced tomatoes, with their juices
1 (6-ounce) can no-salt-added tomato paste

1 teaspoon dried basil
1 teaspoon dried oregano
Salt and pepper to taste
½ teaspoon sugar
1½ cups rice
2 cups water
1 pound medium shrimp, peeled
8 to 10 medium bell peppers

Preheat the oven to 350° F. In a large pot coated with nonstick cooking spray, sauté the onion and garlic over medium heat until tender, about 5 minutes. Add the tomato sauce, tomatoes, tomato paste, basil, oregano, salt and pepper, and sugar. Lower heat and cook for 5 minutes. Add the rice and water. Bring to a boil and simmer, covered, for 10 minutes. Stir in the shrimp and continue cooking, stirring occasionally to prevent sticking, about 10 to 15 minutes, until the shrimp are done. You may have to add more water if it all evaporates before the rice is tender. Meanwhile, slice the tops off of the bell peppers, remove the core, and rinse out the seeds. Place the peppers in a large pot of boiling water for 5 minutes. Remove the peppers from the water and drain. Fill each pepper with the seafood mixture. Place upright in the bottom of a shallow baking dish and bake, uncovered, for 10 to 20 minutes, until well heated.

Makes 8 to 10 servings

Nutritional information per serving

Calories	194	Cal. from Fat (%)	4.3	Sodium (g)	95
Fat (g)	0.9	Saturated Fat (g)	0.2	Cholesterol (mg)	65
Protein (g)	11.3	Carbohydrate (g)	35.3		

Paella

For those of you who usually skip over paella because of the different steps and many pots, my simple version makes it easy for you to serve this wonderful Spanish dish.

1 onion, chopped
1 green bell pepper, seeded and chopped
1 tablespoon minced garlic
2 pounds skinless, boneless chicken breasts, cut into 1½-inch chunks
8 ounces low-fat smoked sausage, cut into ½-inch slices and halved
1½ pounds medium shrimp, peeled
2 medium zucchini, sliced

1 (14½-ounce) can no-salt-added diced tomatoes, with their juices
2 (16-ounce) cans fat-free chicken broth
1 tablespoon paprika
½ teaspoon crushed red pepper flakes
2 cups rice
1 (5-ounce) package saffron yellow long-grain rice
1 (10-ounce) package frozen peas, thawed

In a large pot coated with nonstick cooking spray, sauté the onion, green pepper, garlic, chicken, and sausage over medium-high heat. Cook for 5 to 7 minutes and add the shrimp. Continue to cook until the chicken is done, about 5 to 7 minutes longer. Add the zucchini, tomatoes, chicken broth, paprika, red pepper, rice, and yellow rice mix. Bring to a boil, lower heat, cover, and continue cooking for 20 to 25 minutes, or until the rice is done and the water is absorbed. Fold in the peas and continue cooking for 5 minutes longer, or until well heated.

Makes 12 servings

Nutritional information per serving

Calories	360	Cal. from Fat (%)	8.5	Sodium (g)	687
Fat (g)	3.4	Saturated Fat (g)	1	Cholesterol (mg)	135
Protein (g)	34.8	Carbohydrate (g)	44.9		

Cheesy Shrimp-Rice Casserole

Prepare this incredibly quick shrimp and rice dish with the hint of cheese and salsa once and your family will request it again and again.

1 onion, chopped
1 teaspoon minced garlic
½ cup chopped red or green bell pepper
1½ pounds medium shrimp, peeled
1 (8-ounce) can mushroom stems and pieces
1½ cups shredded reduced-fat Cheddar cheese

⅓ cup salsa
1 tablespoon Worcestershire sauce
½ cup evaporated skimmed milk
1 bunch green onions (scallions), sliced
2 tablespoons canned diced green chilies, drained
3 cups cooked rice

In a large skillet coated with nonstick cooking spray, sauté the onion, garlic, pepper, shrimp, and mushrooms over medium-high heat for about 5 to 7 minutes. Add the Cheddar, salsa, Worcestershire sauce, evaporated milk, green onions, and green chilies. Stir in the rice and cook until the cheese is melted and well combined, about 10 minutes.

Makes 6 servings

Nutritional information per serving

Calories	323	Cal. from Fat (%) 20.6		Sodium (g)	674
Fat (g)	7.4	Saturated Fat (g)	4.4	Cholesterol (mg)	182
Protein (g)	29.4	Carbohydrate (g) 32.4			

Shrimp, Peas, and Rice

This dish gets its personality from an assortment of Chinese ingredients.

1¼ cups rice
1 (14½-ounce) can fat-free chicken broth
1 cup water
1 teaspoon ground ginger
¼ cup reduced-sodium soy sauce

1 pound medium shrimp, peeled
1 (10-ounce) package frozen peas, thawed and drained
1 (8-ounce) can sliced water chestnuts, drained
½ cup sliced green onions (scallions)

Place the rice in a large skillet coated with nonstick cooking spray and cook over medium heat, stirring occasionally, until the rice is golden, about 2 to 3 minutes. Stir in the chicken broth, water, and ginger. Continue cooking until the mixture comes to a full boil. Reduce the heat to low, cover, and continue cooking until the rice is tender and the liquid is absorbed, about 15 minutes. Stir in the soy sauce, shrimp, peas, and water chestnuts. Continue cooking, stirring occasionally, until the shrimp turn pink, about 8 minutes. Stir in the green onions.

Makes 6 servings

Nutritional information per serving

Calories	286	Cal. from Fat (%)	3.7	Sodium (g)	674
Fat (g)	1.2	Saturated Fat (g)	0.3	Cholesterol (mg)	108
Protein (g)	18.8	Carbohydrate (g)	47.9		

Shrimp with Potatoes

This combination of shrimp with potatoes is scrumptious. The water the potatoes cook in is seasoned, so they will be spicy also. If you live in an area where crab boil is available, it can be used to season the water for the potatoes and omit the hot pepper sauce.

2 pounds red potatoes
2 tablespoons hot pepper sauce
Salt and pepper to taste
1 bunch green onions (scallions), chopped
2 cups sliced mushrooms
1 tablespoon minced garlic
1 pound medium shrimp, peeled
1 cup shredded reduced-fat Cheddar cheese

Place the potatoes, hot pepper sauce, and salt and pepper in a large pot and add enough water to cover the potatoes. Bring to a boil and cook the potatoes for 25 minutes, or until tender. Let cool slightly, peel, chop coarsely, and place in an 2-quart oblong casserole dish coated with nonstick cooking spray. Preheat the oven to 350° F. In a large pan coated with nonstick cooking spray, sauté the green onions, mushrooms, garlic, and shrimp until the shrimp turn pink, about 5 to 7 minutes. Transfer the shrimp mixture to the top of the potatoes. Sprinkle with the Cheddar and bake for 10 minutes, until the cheese is melted and bubbly.

Makes 4 to 6 servings

Nutritional information per serving

Calories	237	Cal. from Fat (%)	18.7	Sodium (g)	586
Fat (g)	4.9	Saturated Fat (g)	2.9	Cholesterol (mg)	121
Protein (g)	10.4	Carbohydrate (g)	28.8		

Shrimp and Chicken Étouffée

Étouffée means the shrimp and chicken are smothered with a highly seasoned tomato-based sauce.

½ cup all-purpose flour
1½ pounds skinless, boneless chicken breasts, cut into 1½-inch chunks
1 onion, chopped
1 green bell pepper, seeded and chopped
½ cup chopped celery
1 teaspoon minced garlic
1 (6-ounce) can no-salt-added tomato paste

1 (16-ounce) can fat-free chicken broth
1 bay leaf
1 teaspoon dried thyme
¼ teaspoon pepper
1 pound medium shrimp, peeled
¼ cup chopped parsley
½ cup chopped green onions (scallions)
4 cups cooked rice

Preheat the oven to 400° F. Spread the flour on a baking sheet and bake, stirring occasionally, for 25 minutes, or until golden brown. Set aside. In a large pot coated with nonstick cooking spray, brown the chicken over medium heat, about 7 minutes. Add the onion, bell pepper, celery, and garlic, sautéing until tender, about 7 minutes. Stir in the browned flour, tomato paste, chicken broth, bay leaf, thyme, pepper, and shrimp and cook for 6 minutes. Stir in the parsley and green onions and cook for 3 minutes more. Serve over the rice.

Makes 6 servings

Nutritional information per serving

Calories	412	Cal. from Fat (%)	9.4	Sodium (g)	403
Fat (g)	4.3	Saturated Fat (g)	1.1	Cholesterol (mg)	177
Protein (g)	43.2	Carbohydrate (g)	47.4		

Scallops in Tarragon Sauce

The creamy, rich sauce with pasta will appeal to the gourmet.

1 (16-ounce) package vermicelli pasta
1 pound mushrooms, sliced
1 bunch green onions (scallions), sliced
1 teaspoon minced garlic
2 pounds bay scallops

⅓ cup dry white wine
2 tablespoons lemon juice
1 tablespoon dried tarragon
Salt and pepper to taste
1 cup nonfat sour cream
¼ cup all-purpose flour
Chopped parsley (optional)

Cook the pasta according to package directions, omitting any oil and salt. Drain and set aside. In a large skillet coated with nonstick cooking spray, sauté the mushrooms, green onions, and garlic over medium-high heat until tender, about 5 minutes. Add the scallops, wine, lemon juice, tarragon, and salt and pepper. Cook over low heat 5 minutes, or until the scallops are opaque. Combine the sour cream and flour together. Stir into the scallop mixture, cooking until the sauce begins to thicken, about 3 to 5 minutes. Do not boil. Serve over the pasta and sprinkle with the parsley, if desired.

Makes 8 servings

Nutritional information per serving

Calories	399	Cal. from Fat (%)	5.2	Sodium (g)	231
Fat (g)	2.3	Saturated Fat (g)	0.3	Cholesterol (mg)	42
Protein (g)	29.8	Carbohydrate (g)	60.7		

Red Snapper Dill Divan

The fabulous cheesy dill sauce makes this one dish to remember.

5 cups broccoli florets
½ cup water
1½ pounds red snapper fillets (or any other firm-textured fish fillets)
Salt and pepper to taste

2 tablespoons all-purpose flour
1½ cups skim milk
⅓ cup shredded reduced-fat Cheddar cheese
1 teaspoon dried dillweed

Preheat the oven to 425° F. Cook the broccoli in the water in a covered microwaveproof dish for 5 minutes in the microwave. Drain well and place the broccoli in an 2-quart oblong baking dish. Place the fish in a single layer over the broccoli. Sprinkle the fish with salt and pepper. Place the flour in a small saucepan, gradually add the milk, and cook, stirring constantly, until thickened, about 3 to 5 minutes. Stir in the Cheddar, the dillweed, and salt and pepper, stirring until the cheese is melted. Pour the cheese mixture over the fish. Bake, uncovered, for 15 to 20 minutes, or until the fish flakes easily.

Makes 4 servings

Nutritional information per serving

Calories	265	Cal. from Fat (%)	16.1	Sodium (g)	229
Fat (g)	4.7	Saturated Fat (g)	2	Cholesterol (mg)	66
Protein (g)	41.4	Carbohydrate (g)	13.6		

Snapper-Vegetable Gratin

Everyone loves gratins, and with the fish and vegetables, this popular dish becomes a meal.

1 pound red snapper fillets	½ cup reserved fish stock
½ teaspoon pepper, divided	(from cooking the fish)
½ cup dry white wine	2 tablespoons minced green
2 small zucchini, thinly	onions (scallions)
sliced	¼ teaspoon crushed red
1 yellow squash, thinly sliced	pepper flakes
1 large red bell pepper,	1 cup skim milk
seeded and chopped	¼ cup all-purpose flour
1 pound sliced mushrooms	½ cup chopped parsley
1 teaspoon dried basil	½ cup shredded reduced-fat
1 teaspoon dried oregano	Cheddar cheese

Preheat the oven to 400° F. Sprinkle the fillets with ¼ teaspoon of the pepper. Place the fillets in a 13 × 9 × 2-inch baking dish coated with nonstick cooking spray. Pour the wine over the fillets. Bake, uncovered, for 10 to 12 minutes, or until the fish flakes easily when tested with a fork. Drain the fish, reserving ½ cup of the clear cooking liquid; set aside. In a large skillet coated with nonstick cooking spray, sauté the zucchini, squash, red pepper, and mushrooms over medium-high heat until tender, about 5 to 8 minutes. Stir in the basil, oregano, and remaining pepper. Spoon the mixture over the fillets. Combine the reserved liquid, green onions, and red pepper in a saucepan. Bring to a boil, reduce the heat, and simmer until the green onions are tender, about 2 minutes. Combine the milk and flour in a small bowl and add to the saucepan. Cook, stirring constantly, 2 minutes, or until the sauce thickens. Remove from the heat. Stir in the parsley. Spoon the sauce over the vegetables and fillets. Sprinkle with the Cheddar and bake for 5 minutes, or until the cheese is melted and bubbly.

Makes 4 servings

Nutritional information per serving

Calories	284	Cal. from Fat (%) 17.5		Sodium (g)	214
Fat (g)	5.5	Saturated Fat (g) 2.6		Cholesterol (mg)	50
Protein (g)	32.2	Carbohydrate (g) 22.6			

Fish Florentine

Any fresh, mild fish can be used, such as flounder, trout, or orange roughy. The creamy spinach topped with the dill-seasoned fish is a delicious dish and an attractive presentation.

2 (10-ounce) packages frozen chopped spinach	½ cup nonfat sour cream
¼ cup all-purpose flour	2 pounds fish fillets
1 cup skim milk	1 teaspoon dried dillweed
½ cup canned fat-free chicken broth	Salt and pepper to taste
	2 tablespoons lemon juice

Preheat the oven to 350° F. Cook the spinach according to package directions. Drain very well; set aside. Place the flour in a small saucepan and gradually whisk in the milk and chicken broth. Cook over medium heat until thickened, stirring, about 5 minutes Remove from the heat and fold in the sour cream. Stir 1 cup of the sauce into the spinach, mixing well. Spread the creamed spinach on the bottom of a 2-quart casserole dish coated with nonstick cooking spray. Arrange the fish fillets over the spinach. Sprinkle the fish with the dillweed and salt and pepper and drizzle with the lemon juice. Pour the remaining sauce over the fish. Bake, covered with foil, for 30 minutes, or until the fish is done and flakes easily when tested with a fork.

Makes 4 servings

Nutritional information per serving

Calories	314	Cal. from Fat (%)	8.7	Sodium (g)	417
Fat (g)	3.1	Saturated Fat (g)	0.7	Cholesterol (mg)	122
Protein (g)	48.8	Carbohydrate (g)	20.7		

Mediterranean Catch

The Greek influence in this dish makes it popular. I love feta cheese, and when it is combined with tomatoes, the colors are very appealing. Choose your favorite fish fillets.

1 large onion, sliced
1 large green bell pepper, seeded and cut into thin strips
1 cup sliced Roma (plum) tomatoes
1 tablespoon minced garlic
2 pounds firm textured fish fillets (such as redfish, snapper, grouper)

Salt and pepper to taste
1 teaspoon dried oregano
6 ounces feta cheese, crumbled
1 tablespoon chopped parsley (optional)
12 ounces angel hair (capellini) pasta

Preheat the oven to 375° F. In a large skillet coated with nonstick cooking spray, sauté the onion and green pepper over medium heat until tender, about 5 minutes. Add the tomatoes and garlic, stirring for several more minutes. Arrange the fish in a single layer in a 3-quart oblong baking dish. Season with salt and pepper and sprinkle with the oregano. Spoon the vegetable mixture over the seasoned fish. Sprinkle with the feta. Bake for 20 to 25 minutes, or until the fish flakes easily with a fork. Sprinkle with parsley. Meanwhile, prepare the pasta according to the package directions, omitting any oil and salt. Drain and serve the fish and sauce on top of the pasta.

Makes 6 servings

Nutritional information per serving

Calories	468	Cal. from Fat (%)	17.7	Sodium (g)	385
Fat (g)	9.2	Saturated Fat (g)	4.8	Cholesterol (mg)	76
Protein (g)	41.3	Carbohydrate (g)	52.9		

Pizza-Baked Fish

Now you can have all the appealing flavors of pizza in a fish dish. Use your favorite fish instead of the red snapper, if you like.

½ pound sliced mushrooms,
  divided
⅔ cup chopped onion
½ teaspoon minced garlic
¾ cup water
½ cup no-salt-added tomato
  paste
1 teaspoon dried basil
1 teaspoon dried oregano

¼ teaspoon sugar
⅛ teaspoon crushed red
  pepper flakes
2 pounds red snapper fillets
1 green bell pepper, seeded
  and sliced into rings
1 cup shredded part-skim
  mozzarella cheese

Preheat the oven to 400° F. In a skillet coated with nonstick cooking spray, combine half the mushrooms and all the onion and garlic, and sauté over medium heat until tender, about 5 minutes. Add the water, tomato paste, basil, oregano, sugar, and red pepper. Bring to a boil, reduce the heat, and simmer, uncovered, for 5 minutes, stirring occasionally. Remove from the heat. Place the fish in an 2-quart oblong baking dish coated with nonstick cooking spray and pour the sauce over the fish. Top with the remaining mushrooms and the pepper rings. Bake the fish for 15 minutes. Sprinkle with the mozzarella and continue baking for 5 minutes, or until the fish flakes with a fork and the cheese is melted.

Makes 6 servings

Nutritional information per serving

Calories	228	Cal. from Fat (%)	21.1	Sodium (g)	168
Fat (g)	5.3	Saturated Fat (g)	2.4	Cholesterol (mg)	62
Protein (g)	35.2	Carbohydrate (g)	9.3		

Baked Stuffed Fish with Cheese Sauce ♥

Spinach topped with an old-fashioned stuffing layered with fish and a cheese sauce will satisy the hungriest of diners. This recipe works with any fish, so use what is available in your area. Add crabmeat to the stuffing for the deluxe version.

2 (10-ounce) packages
frozen chopped spinach
Salt and pepper to taste
½ cup chopped onion
1 teaspoon minced garlic
½ cup chopped celery
⅓ cup chopped green onions
(scallions)
½ cup chopped green bell
pepper
1 cup seasoned stuffing mix
½ cup canned fat-free
chicken broth

¼ teaspoon dried sage
½ teaspoon dried thyme
2 pounds fish fillets
¼ cup lemon juice
2 tablespoons all-purpose
flour
1 cup skim milk
½ cup shredded reduced-fat
sharp Cheddar cheese
Paprika

Preheat the oven to 350° F. Cook the spinach according to the package directions; drain very well. Place the spinach along the bottom of a 2-quart casserole dish. Sprinkle with salt and pepper. Meanwhile, in a skillet coated with nonstick cooking spray, sauté the onion, garlic, celery, green onion, and green pepper over medium-high heat until tender, about 5 to 7 minutes. Add the stuffing mix, chicken broth, sage, and thyme, mixing well. Spread the stuffing evenly over the spinach. Place the fish fillets in one layer over the stuffing. Sprinkle with the lemon juice and salt and pepper. Place the flour in a small saucepan and gradually mix in the milk. Bring to a boil, stirring constantly, over medium-high heat and continue cooking until the mixture thickens, about 5 minutes. Reduce the heat and stir in the Cheddar until melted. Pour the cheese sauce over the fish and sprinkle the top with paprika. Bake, uncovered, for 30 minutes, or until the fish is done and flakes easily when tested with a fork.

Makes 6 servings

Nutritional information per serving

Calories	293	Cal. from Fat (%)	14.8	Sodium (g)	549
Fat (g)	4.8	Saturated Fat (g)	2	Cholesterol (mg)	59
Protein (g)	37.4	Carbohydrate (g)	24.3		

Baked Fish on Rice Pilaf

This colorful fish dish is a great choice when you have fresh fish and need a new idea. You can omit the cheese if you like.

½ pound sliced fresh
   mushrooms
1 cup chopped onion
3 cups cooked rice
2 tablespoons chopped
   parsley
1 (2-ounce) jar diced
   pimientos, drained
1½ pounds flounder or other
   fillets

¼ cup balsamic vinegar
2 tablespoons lemon juice
⅓ cup dry white wine
Salt and pepper to taste
2 tomatoes, thinly sliced
⅔ cup shredded reduced-fat
   Cheddar cheese

Preheat the oven to 350° F. In a skillet coated with nonstick cooking spray, sauté the mushrooms and onion until tender, about 8 minutes. Stir in the rice, parsley, and pimientos, mixing well. Turn out into a shallow 2-quart casserole coated with nonstick cooking spray. Arrange the fillets on top of the rice mixture. Combine the vinegar, lemon juice, and wine and pour over the fish. Season with salt and pepper. Bake for 15 minutes. Cover the fillets with the tomato slices and continue baking for 5 minutes. Sprinkle with the Cheddar and bake another 5 minutes, or until fillets are white and flaky, and the cheese is melted.

Makes 6 servings

Nutritional information per serving

Calories	281	Cal. from Fat (%)	14.6	Sodium (g)	205
Fat (g)	4.6	Saturated Fat (g)	2.2	Cholesterol (mg)	65
Protein (g)	26.6	Carbohydrate (g)	30.2		

Crawfish Jambalaya

If crawfish tails are not available, substitute peeled shrimp. Jambalaya is a marvelous Cajun rice dish descended from Spanish paella.

1 tablespoon minced garlic	2 ounces Canadian bacon,
1½ cups chopped onion	chopped
1 cup chopped green bell	2 tablespoons chopped
pepper	parsley
1 (10-ounce) can diced	1 cup sliced green onions
tomatoes and green	(scallions)
chilies, with their juices	Salt and pepper to taste
1 pound peeled crawfish	3 cups cooked rice
tails, rinsed	

In a large skillet coated with nonstick cooking spray, sauté the garlic, onion, and green pepper over medium heat until tender, about 5 minutes. Add the chopped tomatoes and chilies. Add the crawfish tails and Canadian bacon, cooking over medium heat for 10 minutes. Add the parsley, green onions, and salt and pepper. Cook 1 minute longer to heat well. Stir in the rice and mix well.

Makes 6 servings

Nutritional information per serving

Calories	218	Cal. from Fat (%)	8.4	Sodium (g)	413
Fat (g)	2	Saturated Fat (g)	0.5	Cholesterol (mg)	108
Protein (g)	18.7	Carbohydrate (g)	30.5		

Crawfish and Rice Casserole

You can substitute shrimp in this crowd-pleasing dish.

1 (8-ounce) package light	4 ounces light pasteurized
cream cheese, cubed	processed cheese spread,
2 tablespoons light stick	cubed
margarine	6 cups cooked rice
2 large onions, chopped	2 bunches green onions
2 large green bell peppers,	(scallions), chopped
seeded and chopped	1 teaspoon minced garlic
2 pounds crawfish tails, rinsed	¼ teaspoon cayenne pepper
1 (10½-ounce) can reduced-	Dash of white pepper
fat cream of mushroom	
soup	

Preheat the oven to 350° F. In the microwave, melt the cream cheese in a microwaveproof dish for 1 minute, stirring until melted; set aside. In a large skillet, melt the margarine over medium heat and sauté the onions and peppers until tender, about 5 minutes. Add the crawfish tails and cook 10 minutes, or until well heated. Add the cream of mushroom soup, cream cheese, cheese spread, cooked rice, green onions, garlic, cayenne, and white pepper. Transfer to a 2- to 3-quart casserole dish coated with nonstick cooking spray. Bake, uncovered, for 30 minutes.

Makes 12 to 16 servings

Nutritional information per serving

Calories	213	Cal. from Fat (%) 23.5		Sodium (g)	338
Fat (g)	5.6	Saturated Fat (g) 2.5		Cholesterol (mg)	90
Protein (g)	15.5	Carbohydrate (g) 24.7			

Crabmeat au Gratin

If you like, top this super casserole with shredded reduced-fat Cheddar cheese before baking.

6 tablespoons light stick margarine	$\frac{1}{8}$ teaspoon cayenne pepper
$\frac{1}{2}$ cup chopped celery	1 (12-ounce) can evaporated skimmed milk
1 onion, chopped	$\frac{1}{3}$ cup skim milk
1 bunch green onions (scallions), green part only, sliced	2 pounds lump or white crabmeat, or combination of both
$\frac{1}{3}$ cup all-purpose flour	$\frac{1}{4}$ cup dry bread crumbs

Preheat the oven to 350° F. In a medium pot, melt the margarine over medium heat and sauté the celery, onion, and green onion stems until tender, about 5 minutes. Add the flour and cayenne, stirring. Gradually add the evaporated milk and skim milk and cook, stirring, until the mixture thickens. Gently fold in the crabmeat. Place in a casserole dish coated with nonstick cooking spray or in individual sprayed ramekins. Sprinkle with the bread crumbs. Bake for 10 minutes.

Makes 6 to 8 servings

Nutritional information per serving

Calories	254	Cal. from Fat (%) 29.9		Sodium (g)	506
Fat (g)	8.4	Saturated Fat (g) 1.5		Cholesterol (mg)	115
Protein (g)	28.4	Carbohydrate (g) 15.2			

Crabmeat and Artichoke Pasta Casserole

If white or lump crabmeat is too expensive or not available, claw crabmeat, imitation crabmeat, or canned crabmeat can be substituted. This tasty casserole has a fancy flair with the crabmeat, artichokes, and Madeira wine.

1 tablespoon light stick margarine
½ cup finely chopped onion
⅓ cup all-purpose flour
¼ cup skim milk
1 (12-ounce) can evaporated skimmed milk
¼ cup Madeira wine
Salt and pepper to taste
1 tablespoon lemon juice
1 pound lump or white crabmeat, picked over for any pieces of shell

1 (8-ounce) package shell pasta
1 (14-ounce) can quartered artichoke hearts, drained
½ cup shredded reduced-fat Cheddar cheese
½ cup sliced green onions (scallions)

Preheat the oven to 350° F. In a large pot coated with nonstick cooking spray, melt the margarine and sauté the onion over medium-high heat until golden, about 3 minutes. Stir in the flour. Gradually add the skim milk and evaporated milk, stirring constantly. Heat and stir until the sauce comes to a boil. Reduce the heat and add the wine. Season with salt and pepper. Drizzle the lemon juice over the crabmeat in a bowl, tossing lightly. Meanwhile, prepare the pasta according to package directions, omitting any oil and salt; drain. Combine the crabmeat, artichoke hearts, pasta, and sauce together in a 3-quart casserole dish coated with nonstick cooking spray. Sprinkle the top with Cheddar and green onions. Bake for 20 minutes, or until the cheese is melted and the casserole is heated through.

Makes 4 servings

Nutritional information per serving

Calories	568	Cal. from Fat (%) 13.6		Sodium (g)	791
Fat (g)	8.6	Saturated Fat (g)	3	Cholesterol (mg)	127
Protein (g)	45.3	Carbohydrate (g) 73.8			

PASTA

Chicken and Artichoke Vermicelli

A true winner—one of my family's favorites! The wonderful sauce and the paprika coloring make it so appetizing. I used lots of pepper because in my house everyone likes spicy dishes.

2 pounds skinless, boneless chicken breasts, cut into large strips
1 tablespoon paprika
Salt and pepper to taste
1 (14-ounce) can quartered artichoke hearts, drained
1/4 cup all-purpose flour
1 (14 1/2-ounce) can fat-free

chicken broth
1/2 cup dry sherry
1 teaspoon dried rosemary
1 (16-ounce) package vermicelli pasta
1/3 cup green onions (scallions), green part only, sliced

Preheat the oven to 350° F. Lay the chicken breasts in a 3-quart oblong baking dish coated with nonstick cooking spray. Season with paprika and salt and pepper. Place the artichokes around the chicken. Place the flour in a saucepan and gradually stir in the chicken broth. Cook over medium heat until thickened, about 3 to 5 minutes. Add the sherry and rosemary and continue cooking for 1 minute. Pour over the seasoned chicken breasts. Bake, covered, for 1 hour. Meanwhile, prepare the pasta according to package directions, omitting any oil and salt. Drain and toss with the green onions. Serve with the chicken and sauce.

Makes 6 to 8 servings

Nutritional information per serving

Calories	420	Cal. from Fat (%)	9	Sodium (g)	284
Fat (g)	4.2	Saturated Fat (g)	1	Cholesterol (mg)	69
Protein (g)	35	Carbohydrate (g)	54.6		

Chicken Oregano with Angel Hair

Everyone loves a delicious red sauce. If the sauce gets too thick, add a little water.

1½ pounds skinless, boneless chicken breasts
1 onion, chopped
½ teaspoon minced garlic
Salt and pepper to taste
1 tablespoon dried oregano
1 (16-ounce) can no-salt-added whole tomatoes, crushed, with their juices

½ pound mushrooms, sliced
¼ cup dry red wine (optional)
1 (8-ounce) package angel hair (capellini) pasta
1 tablespoon olive oil
1 tablespoon chopped parsley

In a large skillet coated with nonstick cooking spray, brown the chicken on both sides over medium heat, about 5 minutes in all, cooking in batches if necessary. Add the onion and garlic and cook 5 minutes more, or until the vegetables are tender. Sprinkle with salt and pepper and oregano. Add the tomatoes, mushrooms, and wine, if desired. Cover and cook over low heat about 20 minutes, or until the chicken is tender. Meanwhile, prepare the pasta according to package directions, omitting any oil and salt. Drain and mix with the olive oil and parsley. Serve the chicken and sauce over the pasta.

Makes 4 to 6 servings

Nutritional information per serving

Calories	335	Cal. from Fat (%)	16.5	Sodium (g)	70
Fat (g)	6.2	Saturated Fat (g)	1.3	Cholesterol (mg)	69
Protein (g)	32.1	Carbohydrate (g)	36.4		

Orzo Paella

In this dish orzo, the rice-shaped pasta, takes on the flavors of paella. Fish, scallops, or any substitutions can be made, according to your preference.

8 ounces low-fat smoked
sausage, thinly sliced
1½ pounds skinless, boneless
chicken breasts, cut into
1½-inch chunks
1 onion, chopped
1 green bell pepper, seeded
and chopped
1 tablespoon minced garlic
1 pound medium shrimp,
peeled

1 (8-ounce) can no-salt-
added tomato sauce
½ teaspoon crushed red
pepper flakes
1 tomato, chopped
1 (16-ounce) package orzo
pasta
1 (10-ounce) package frozen
green peas, thawed
½ cup chopped green onions
(scallions)

In a large pan coated with nonstick cooking spray, cook the sausage over medium-high heat, stirring constantly, until lightly browned, about 3 minutes. Add the chicken and continue cooking, stirring constantly, until the chicken is lightly browned, about 6 minutes. Add the onion, green pepper, and garlic and sauté, stirring constantly, until the vegetables are tender, about 5 to 7 minutes. Add the shrimp, tomato sauce, red pepper, and tomato and cook for 5 to 10 minutes, or until the shrimp are done and the chicken is tender. Meanwhile, prepare the pasta according to package directions, omitting any oil and salt. Drain and add to the chicken mixture, tossing well. Stir in the peas and green onions and continue cooking until well heated, about 5 minutes.

Makes 6 to 8 servings

Nutritional information per serving

Calories	826	Cal. from Fat (%)	7.1	Sodium (g)	388
Fat (g)	6.5	Saturated Fat (g)	1	Cholesterol (mg)	145
Protein (g)	60.8	Carbohydrate (g)	126.3		

Greek Shrimp Orzo

Orzo is a rice-shaped pasta, available in your pasta section. My kids love the flavors of this dish and they always ask for seconds.

1 cup chopped onion
1 tablespoon minced garlic
¼ cup dry white wine
1 (28-ounce) can no-salt-added whole tomatoes, chopped, with their juices
2 tablespoons chopped parsley
2 tablespoons drained capers

1 teaspoon dried oregano
1 teaspoon dried basil
Salt and pepper to taste
Dash of crushed red pepper flakes
1½ pounds medium shrimp, peeled
1½ cups orzo pasta
½ cup crumbled feta cheese

Preheat the oven to 450° F. In a 2-quart saucepan coated with non-stick cooking spray, cook the onion and garlic over medium heat, sautéing for 3 minutes, or until tender. Add the wine and boil for about 1 minute. Stir in the tomatoes, parsley, capers, oregano, basil, salt and pepper, and red pepper and cook for 5 minutes. Add the shrimp and cook, stirring, for 5 minutes, or just until the shrimp turn pink. Meanwhile, cook the pasta according to package directions, omitting any oil and salt. Drain and place in a shallow 2-quart casserole dish. Toss with the tomato-shrimp sauce, sprinkle with the feta, and bake, uncovered, for 10 minutes, or until the cheese is well heated.

Makes 4 to 6 servings

Nutritional information per serving

Calories	474	Cal. from Fat (%)	12.8	Sodium (g)	543
Fat (g)	6.8	Saturated Fat (g)	3.3	Cholesterol (mg)	180
Protein (g)	34.4	Carbohydrate (g)	64.3		

PASTA

Shrimp with Oranges and Pasta

With the hint of Brie cheese and orange, the impression you'll make with this gourmet dish will be memorable—and with hardly any fuss. Put this high on your list!

1 (16-ounce) package
 mostaccioli, ziti, or any
 other tubular pasta
1 red onion, sliced
1 teaspoon chopped
 jalapeño pepper
2 pounds medium shrimp,
 peeled

1 teaspoon minced garlic
½ cup orange juice
2 oranges, separated into
 segments
1 teaspoon dried basil
6 ounces Brie cheese, rind
 removed, cut into chunks

Cook the pasta according to package directions, omitting oil and salt. Drain; set aside. In a large skillet coated with nonstick cooking spray, sauté the onion, jalapeño, shrimp, and garlic until the shrimp are done, about 5 to 8 minutes. Add the orange juice, orange segments, and basil, stirring well, and cook just until heated through. Toss the pasta with the shrimp sauce and add the Brie, stirring gently, until the cheese is melted.

Makes 6 servings

Nutritional information per serving

Calories	517	Cal. from Fat (%) 16.1	Sodium (g)	406
Fat (g)	9.3	Saturated Fat (g) 4.6	Cholesterol (mg)	239
Protein (g)	38.7	Carbohydrate (g) 67.7		

Creamy Shrimp with Vermicelli

The subtle flavor of dill in this pasta dish is very welcoming. This recipe proves that a dish can taste good without tons of seasoning.

1 tablespoon light stick
 margarine
¼ cup all-purpose flour
2 cups skim milk
1 tablespoon lemon juice
1 teaspoon dried dillweed
1½ pounds medium shrimp,
 peeled

1 (12-ounce) package
 vermicelli pasta
¼ cup grated Parmesan
 cheese (optional)
Salt and pepper to taste

124

In a saucepan, melt the margarine over low heat and blend in the flour. Gradually add the milk; cook, stirring constantly, until the mixture thickens, about 3 minutes. Add the lemon juice, dillweed, and shrimp, stirring. Cook over medium heat until the shrimp turn pink, about 5 to 7 minutes. Meanwhile, prepare the pasta according to package directions, omitting any oil and salt. Drain. Serve the shrimp and sauce over the pasta. Sprinkle with Parmesan, if desired. Season with salt and pepper.

Makes 4 to 6 servings

Nutritional information per serving

Calories	367	Cal. from Fat (%)	8.6	Sodium (g)	250
Fat (g)	3.5	Saturated Fat (g)	0.7	Cholesterol (mg)	163
Protein (g)	28.3	Carbohydrate (g)	53.5		

Shrimp Rosemary and Pasta

The tomatoes and green onions make this very quick dish attractive, while the rosemary and sherry give it distinction.

1 (16-ounce) package angel hair (capellini) pasta
2 pounds medium shrimp, peeled
1 tablespoon minced garlic
1 tablespoon dried rosemary
¼ teaspoon pepper
½ cup sherry
1 cup chopped fresh Roma (plum) tomatoes
1 bunch green onions (scallions), thinly sliced
2 tablespoons chopped parsley

Cook the pasta according to package directions, omitting any oil and salt. Drain; set aside. In a large skillet coated with nonstick cooking spray, cook the shrimp and garlic until the shrimp turn pink, about 5 minutes. Add the rosemary, pepper, sherry, tomatoes, green onions, and parsley and sauté for 3 to 4 minutes, until the shrimp are done. Add the pasta and toss well.

Makes 6 to 8 servings

Nutritional information per serving

Calories	345	Cal. from Fat (%)	5.6	Sodium (g)	194
Fat (g)	2.2	Saturated Fat (g)	0.4	Cholesterol (mg)	161
Protein (g)	25.6	Carbohydrate (g)	50.2		

Shrimp and Tomato Pasta

Even though this dish is prepared in minutes, the shrimp and capers make it special. I use fresh Roma tomatoes, but in a pinch you can use canned tomatoes. If you're not a big caper fan, you can reduce the amount in the dish, but I do recommend adding some for flavor.

1 (16-ounce) package angel hair (capellini) pasta
2 pounds medium shrimp, peeled
1 teaspoon minced garlic
2 cups chopped Roma (plum) tomatoes (about 6)
1 tablespoon chopped parsley

½ teaspoon dried thyme
½ teaspoon dried basil
½ teaspoon dried oregano
1½ teaspoons Dijon mustard
3 tablespoons lemon juice
¼ cup capers, drained
Salt and pepper to taste

Prepare the pasta according to package directions, omitting any oil and salt. Drain and set aside. Meanwhile, in a large pan coated with nonstick cooking spray, sauté the shrimp, garlic, tomatoes, parsley, thyme, basil, and oregano over medium heat until the shrimp are done, about 5 to 7 minutes. Mix in the mustard, lemon juice, capers, and salt and pepper. Toss with the pasta and serve.

Makes 6 to 8 servings

Nutritional information per serving

Calories	323	Cal. from Fat (%)	6.2	Sodium (g)	380
Fat (g)	2.2	Saturated Fat (g)	0.4	Cholesterol (mg)	161
Protein (g)	25.5	Carbohydrate (g)	48.1		

Shrimp Ziti Primavera

This pasta dish is well seasoned with Italian spices. Because of the outstanding flavor, you may even leave out the shrimp for a change or a vegetarian meal.

1 (16-ounce) package ziti
(tubular) pasta
2 pounds medium shrimp,
peeled
2 tablespoons minced garlic
1 bunch green onions
(scallions), sliced
1 pound fresh asparagus
spears, cut into 2-inch
pieces
½ pound mushrooms, sliced
2 cups chopped tomatoes

Salt and pepper to taste
⅛ teaspoon crushed red
pepper flakes
½ cup dry white wine
1 tablespoon dried basil
1 tablespoon dried oregano
1 tablespoon dried thyme
¼ cup grated Parmesan
cheese
1 tablespoon chopped
parsley

Cook the pasta according to package directions, omitting any oil and salt. Drain; set aside. Heat a large skillet coated with nonstick cooking spray and cook the shrimp, garlic, and green onions, stirring constantly, until the shrimp turn pink, about 3 minutes. Add the asparagus, mushrooms, tomatoes, salt and pepper, red pepper, wine, basil, oregano, and thyme to the skillet and continue cooking until the shrimp are done and the vegetables are tender, about 5 to 7 minutes. Add the pasta, Parmesan, and parsley, tossing well.

Makes 8 servings

Nutritional information per serving

Calories	365	Cal. from Fat (%)	8	Sodium (g)	245
Fat (g)	3.2	Saturated Fat (g)	1	Cholesterol (mg)	163
Protein (g)	28.7	Carbohydrate (g)	53.2		

Shrimp Pasta Thai Time

If you're not familiar with Thai food, this is the perfect introduction. It will win you over in just seconds.

2 pounds medium shrimp, peeled
1 (8-ounce) bottle fat-free Italian dressing, divided
1 tablespoon reduced-fat peanut butter
1 tablespoon reduced-sodium soy sauce
1 tablespoon honey
1 teaspoon ground ginger

$\frac{1}{4}$ teaspoon crushed red pepper flakes
1 cup shredded peeled carrots
1 cup chopped green onions (scallions)
1 (8-ounce) package angel hair (capellini) pasta
$\frac{1}{4}$ cup chopped fresh cilantro (optional)

In a bowl, mix the shrimp with $\frac{1}{3}$ cup Italian dressing. Refrigerate for 1 hour. In a small bowl, whisk together with a fork the peanut butter, soy sauce, honey, ginger, red pepper, and the remaining dressing; set aside. Drain and discard the dressing from the shrimp. In a large skillet coated with nonstick cooking spray, sauté the shrimp, carrots, and green onions until the shrimp are done, about 5 to 7 minutes. Meanwhile, prepare the pasta according to package directions, omitting any oil and salt. Drain. Add the dressing mixture and pasta to the skillet, tossing until the mixture is well mixed and heated. If desired, sprinkle with cilantro.

Makes 4 to 6 servings

Nutritional information per serving

Calories	318	Cal. from Fat (%)	8.5	Sodium (g)	703
Fat (g)	3	Saturated Fat (g)	0.6	Cholesterol (mg)	215
Protein (g)	29.5	Carbohydrate (g)	41.1		

Orange Roughy Florentine Fettuccine ♡

Dill, spinach, and fish are the perfect combination. Orange roughy is a lean, mild-flavored fish available at your local grocery or seafood market.

1 cup chopped onion
1 teaspoon minced garlic
1 tablespoon cornstarch
1 (12-ounce) can evaporated
   skimmed milk
1 teaspoon dried dillweed
Salt and pepper to taste
3 cups tightly packed,
   coarsely chopped fresh
   spinach (stems removed)

2 pounds orange roughy
   fillets, cut into bite-size
   pieces
1 (12-ounce) package
   fettuccine pasta

In a large skillet coated with nonstick cooking spray, sauté the onion and garlic over medium heat until tender, about 5 minutes. Stir in the cornstarch and immediately add the evaporated milk, stirring until well blended. Add the dillweed and salt and pepper. Continue stirring over medium heat until the mixture thickens, about 5 minutes. Add the spinach, stirring to mix with the sauce, and then the orange roughy. Cook over medium heat until the orange roughy is done and the spinach is wilted, about 5 minutes. Stir occasionally— but carefully, not to break up the fish. Meanwhile, prepare the pasta according to package directions, omitting any oil and salt. Drain. Serve the fish and sauce over the pasta.

Makes 6 servings

Nutritional information per serving

Calories	389	Cal. from Fat (%)	5.5	Sodium (g)	196
Fat (g)	2.4	Saturated Fat (g)	0.3	Cholesterol (mg)	34
Protein (g)	35.9	Carbohydrate (g)	54.1		

Salmon Fettuccine

The two kinds of salmon combined with the tarragon and light sauce give this winning dish lots of pizzazz as well as a great texture.

1 (16-ounce) package
fettuccine or linguine
pasta
1 pound fresh salmon steaks,
skinned, boned, and cut
into ½-inch slices
1 bunch green onions
(scallions), chopped
1 cup coarsely chopped
tomatoes
½ cup dry white wine

½ cup bottled clam juice
1 tablespoon dried tarragon
4 ounces fat-free cream
cheese
4 ounces thinly sliced
smoked salmon, cut into
2-inch strips
Salt and pepper to taste
2 tablespoons chopped
parsley

Cook the pasta according to package directions, omitting any oil and salt. Drain; set aside. In a large skillet coated with nonstick cooking spray, cook the fresh salmon over medium-high heat, tossing until it begins to turn opaque, about 30 seconds. Remove the fish with a slotted spoon; set aside. Add the green onions, tomato, wine, and clam juice to the skillet. Bring to a boil over a high heat until the mixture is slightly thickened, about 5 minutes. Stir in the tarragon and cream cheese, and continue cooking until the sauce thickens slightly, about 2 minutes. Return the salmon to the pan along with any accumulated juices. Stir quickly. As soon as it is heated through, remove from the heat and stir in the smoked salmon. Season with salt and pepper. Pour over the hot pasta. Sprinkle with parsley and serve immediately.

Makes 6 servings

Nutritional information per serving

Calories	433	Cal. from Fat (%)	10.1	Sodium (g)	430
Fat (g)	4.9	Saturated Fat (g)	0.8	Cholesterol (mg)	44
Protein (g)	32.3	Carbohydrate (g)	61.3		

Smoked Salmon and Ziti ♥

Smoked Nova Scotia salmon can be usually found in packages at the grocery store or sometimes in the deli department. You can use fresh asparagus cut in pieces. Just add them to the skillet a little earlier, with the tomatoes, as they will take longer to cook than the canned ones. This is a light, creamy dish.

1 (16-ounce) package ziti or any other tubular pasta
1 cup chopped tomatoes
1 bunch green onions (scallions), chopped
¼ pound sliced smoked Nova Scotia salmon, chopped

1 (15-ounce) can asparagus spears, drained, and cut into thirds
1 tablespoon lemon juice
1 teaspoon dried tarragon
½ cup low-fat ricotta cheese
Salt and pepper to taste

Cook the pasta according to package directions, omitting any oil and salt. Drain; set aside. In a large skillet coated with nonstick cooking spray, sauté the tomato and green onions over medium heat for 2 minutes. Add the smoked salmon, asparagus spears, lemon juice, tarragon, and ricotta and cook, stirring, until the cheese is well blended. Add the pasta, tossing carefully. Season with salt and pepper.

Makes 6 to 8 servings

Nutritional information per serving

Calories	269	Cal. from Fat (%)	8	Sodium (g)	147
Fat (g)	2.4	Saturated Fat (g)	0.7	Cholesterol (mg)	8
Protein (g)	13.7	Carbohydrate (g)	48.6		

Beefy Bow Ties

Sirloin strips, asparagus, and a rich sauce make this special pasta dish welcome on cold winter nights.

1 **pound boneless sirloin steak**	1 **(10¾-ounce) can no-salt-added tomato puree**
1 **pound asparagus, ends trimmed, cut into 2-inches pieces**	1 **teaspoon dried basil**
	¼ **teaspoon pepper**
1 **onion, sliced**	1 **(12-ounce) package bow-tie pasta**
1 **(10½-ounce) can beef broth, divided**	2 **tablespoons grated Parmesan cheese**

Trim any fat from the steak. Cut the steak into 2-inch strips and cut the strips crosswise into ⅛-inch slices. Coat a large skillet with non-stick cooking spray. Heat the skillet over medium heat until hot and cook the asparagus, onion, and 1 cup of the beef broth, stirring occasionally, for 5 to 7 minutes, or until the liquid has almost evaporated; remove the asparagus mixture from the skillet. Put the steak in the same skillet. Cook for about 5 to 7 minutes, stirring frequently, until the steak is no longer pink. Return the asparagus mixture to the skillet. Stir in the remaining broth and the tomato puree, basil, and pepper. Cook for 2 minutes longer, stirring frequently, until the mixture is hot. Meanwhile, cook the pasta according to package directions, omitting any oil and salt. Drain. Serve the steak and asparagus mixture over the pasta. Sprinkle Parmesan over the top.

Makes 6 servings

Nutritional information per serving

Calories	376	Cal. from Fat (%) 16.6		Sodium (g)	242
Fat (g)	6.9	Saturated Fat (g) 2.6		Cholesterol (mg)	47
Protein (g)	25.6	Carbohydrate (g) 52.4			

Meat Sauce with Angel Hair Pasta

One Sunday, my daughter wanted meat sauce with angel hair, so I just used what I had in my pantry and made her very happy. The cheese in the meat sauce is our secret!

2 pounds ground sirloin
1 onion, chopped
1 tablespoon minced garlic
½ pound mushrooms, sliced
1 tablespoon Worcestershire sauce
1 (6-ounce) can no-salt-added tomato paste
2 (16-ounce) cans no-salt-added whole tomatoes, crushed, with their juices

½ teaspoon sugar
1 tablespoon dried oregano
1 tablespoon dried basil
Salt and pepper to taste
⅓ cup dry red wine (optional)
½ cup grated fat-free Parmesan cheese
1 (16-ounce) package angel hair (capellini) pasta

In a large skillet coated with nonstick cooking spray, cook the meat, onion, garlic, and mushrooms over medium-high heat until the meat is done, about 7 minutes. Drain any excess grease. Add the Worcestershire sauce, tomato paste, tomatoes, sugar, oregano, basil, salt and pepper, and wine, if using. Continue cooking for another 15 minutes. Stir in the Parmesan. Meanwhile, cook the pasta according to package directions, omitting any oil and salt. Drain and serve with the meat sauce.

Makes 8 servings

Nutritional information per serving

Calories	466	Cal. from Fat (%)	20.5	Sodium (g)	190
Fat (g)	10.6	Saturated Fat (g)	4.2	Cholesterol (mg)	72
Protein (g)	34.7	Carbohydrate (g)	57		

Italian Meaty Pasta Dish

This quick version of lasagne is great for a crowd of kids—and very nutritious, as it's full of pasta, green beans, and meat.

1 (16-ounce) package ziti
(tubular) pasta
2 pounds ground sirloin
¼ cup chopped parsley
1 onion, finely chopped
1 (26-ounce) can no-salt-
added tomato sauce

1 tablespoon dried basil
1 tablespoon dried oregano
1 (16-ounce) package green
beans, partially thawed
1 cup low-fat ricotta cheese
1 cup shredded part-skim
mozzarella cheese

Cook the pasta according to package directions, omitting any oil and salt. Drain well; set aside. In a large skillet coated with nonstick cooking spray, sauté the meat, parsley, and onion over medium heat, stirring frequently, about 5 to 7 minutes, or until the meat is done. Drain off any excess fat. Stir in the tomato sauce, basil, and oregano, and bring to a simmer. Add the green beans, reduce the heat to low, and simmer, uncovered, for 10 minutes. Stir in the cooked pasta, mixing well. Then place large spoonfuls of the ricotta on top, not touching one another, and sprinkle the mozzarella in between. Cover and cook just until the mozzarella melts and the dish is heated through, about 10 minutes. Do not stir.

Makes 8 to 10 servings

Nutritional information per serving

Calories	399	Cal. from Fat (%)	21.9	Sodium (g)	148
Fat (g)	9.7	Saturated Fat (g)	4.3	Cholesterol (mg)	71
Protein (g)	32.5	Carbohydrate (g)	45.2		

Italian Vegetable and Meat Pasta ♥

This is one of those hearty family dishes that fill up those growing kids. It sneaks in some good vegetables, too.

2 cups ¾-inch cubes peeled eggplant (about 1 pound)
2 cups ¾-inch cubes yellow squash
½ pound small mushrooms
2 tablespoons balsamic vinegar
1½ pounds ground sirloin
1 cup chopped onion
1 teaspoon minced garlic
½ teaspoon crushed red pepper flakes

2 (14½-ounce) cans no-salt-added whole tomatoes, coarsely chopped, with their juices
1 teaspoon dried basil
1 teaspoon dried oregano
1 (16-ounce) package mostaccioli or other tubular pasta
¼ cup grated Parmesan cheese

Preheat the oven to 400° F. Arrange the eggplant, squash, and mushrooms in a single layer on a 15 × 10 × 1-inch jelly-roll pan. Drizzle the vinegar over the vegetables and bake for 8 minutes. Turn the vegetables over and bake an additional 10 minutes, or until the eggplant is tender and lightly browned; set aside. In a large skillet coated with nonstick cooking spray, cook the meat, onion, and garlic over medium heat until the meat is brown, about 8 minutes. Drain any excess grease. Add the red pepper flakes, tomatoes, basil, and oregano. Stir well. Bring to a boil, reduce the heat, and simmer, uncovered, 10 minutes, stirring occasionally. Meanwhile, cook the pasta according to the package directions, omitting any oil and salt. Drain; set aside. Add the vegetable mixture to the meat mixture. Sprinkle with cheese and serve over the pasta.

Makes 8 servings

Nutritional information per serving

Calories	397	Cal. from Fat (%)	17.7	Sodium (g)	96
Fat (g)	7.8	Saturated Fat (g)	2.9	Cholesterol (mg)	53
Protein (g)	27.5	Carbohydrate (g)	53.3		

Manicotti

The creamy filling for this recipe contains all of the all-time best manicotti ingredients—spinach, meat, and cream cheese. A perfect all-in-one dinner. Manicotti freeze well.

16 manicotti shells
1 pound ground sirloin
½ cup chopped onion
2½ teaspoons minced garlic
1 cup low-fat ricotta cheese
1 (8-ounce) package fat-free cream cheese
1 (10-ounce) package frozen chopped spinach, thawed and squeezed dry

1 (28-ounce) can no-salt-added whole tomatoes, chopped, with their juices
1 teaspoon dried oregano
½ teaspoon pepper
Salt to taste
1 teaspoon dried basil

Preheat the oven to 350° F. Cook the manicotti shells according to package directions, omitting any oil and salt. Rinse, drain, and set aside. In a large skillet coated with nonstick cooking spray, cook the meat, onion, and garlic until the meat is done and the vegetables are tender, about 7 minutes. Drain any excess grease. Mix in the ricotta, cream cheese, and spinach. Stuff the shells with the meat mixture and arrange in a baking dish coated with nonstick cooking spray. In a separate bowl, combine the tomatoes, oregano, pepper, salt, and basil. Pour over the shells. Cover and bake for 15 minutes. Uncover and bake for 10 minutes longer, or until bubbly and well heated.

Makes 8 servings

Nutritional information per serving

Calories	247	Cal. from Fat (%)	15.7	Sodium (g)	246
Fat (g)	4.5	Saturated Fat (g)	2	Cholesterol (mg)	49
Protein (g)	25.2	Carbohydrate (g)	29.3		

Chinese Pork Vermicelli

How about a Chinese influence with pasta at home? No need for Chinese take-out!

⅓ cup reduced-sodium soy
  sauce
1 teaspoon ground ginger
¼ teaspoon crushed red
  pepper flakes
1 teaspoon minced garlic
1½ pounds pork tenderloin,
  trimmed of fat and cut into
  1-inch cubes

1 (6-ounce) package frozen
  snow pea pods
1 cup (1½-inch) red bell
  pepper slices
1 (8-ounce) package
  vermicelli pasta
⅓ cup canned fat-free
  chicken broth

Combine the soy sauce, ginger, red pepper flakes, and garlic in a large zip-top heavy-duty plastic bag. Add the pork; seal the bag, shake it, and marinate in the refrigerator for at least 20 minutes. Coat a large skillet with nonstick cooking spray, heat over medium-high heat, add the pork mixture to the skillet, and stir-fry 3 minutes, or until the pork is browned. Add the snow peas and red bell pepper, sautéing until the vegetables are crisp-tender, about 3 to 5 minutes. Meanwhile, cook the pasta according to package directions, omitting any oil and salt. Drain. Add the chicken broth and pasta to the skillet. Cook 1 minute longer, or until heated through.

Makes 6 servings

Nutritional information per serving

Calories	324	Cal. from Fat (%)	16.7	Sodium (g)	526
Fat (g)	6	Saturated Fat (g)	2	Cholesterol (mg)	67
Protein (g)	30.6	Carbohydrate (g)	34.9		

Penne with Spinach, Sun-Dried Tomatoes, and Goat Cheese ♥

When I served this fabulous dish, I felt as if I was at one of those trendy New York restaurants. Don't be alarmed: goat cheese is available at your local grocery store now.

½ cup sun-dried tomatoes
  (not oil-packed)
⅔ cup boiling water
12 ounces penne or other
  tubular pasta
2 tablespoons olive oil
1 tablespoon minced garlic

6 cups stemmed fresh
  spinach, washed
1 tablespoon dried basil
2 tablespoons balsamic
  vinegar
Salt and pepper to taste
½ cup crumbled goat cheese

In a small bowl, combine the sun-dried tomatoes and boiling water and set aside to soften, about 10 minutes. Coarsely chop the sun-dried tomatoes and reserve the soaking liquid. Meanwhile, prepare the pasta according to package directions, omitting any oil and salt. Drain and set aside. In a large skillet coated with nonstick cooking spray, heat the oil and sauté the garlic for 30 seconds. Add the sun-dried tomatoes with their soaking liquid and the spinach, basil, vinegar, and salt and pepper, cooking until the spinach is just wilted, about 5 minutes. Stir in the goat cheese and pasta heating until the cheese is melted.

Makes 4 servings

Nutritional information per serving

Calories	533	Cal. from Fat (%)	30.2	Sodium (g)	340
Fat (g)	17.9	Saturated Fat (g)	7.5	Cholesterol (mg)	24
Protein (g)	20.2	Carbohydrate (g)	73.8		

Tuna Macaroni Casserole

This macaroni casserole with a light dill flavor will attract all tuna fans.

1 (8-ounce) package small elbow or shell pasta
1 onion, chopped
½ cup finely chopped peeled carrot
1 (10¾-ounce) can 98% fat-free cream of mushroom soup
¾ cup skim milk
½ cup chopped green onions (scallions)

½ teaspoon dried dillweed
1 cup frozen peas
1 (12-ounce) can solid white tuna packed in spring water, drained and broken into chunks
⅓ cup crushed low-sodium shredded-wheat crackers
1 tablespoon grated Parmesan cheese

Preheat the oven to 375° F. Cook the pasta according to package directions, omitting any oil and salt. In a skillet coated with nonstick cooking spray, sauté the onion and carrot over medium heat until tender, about 5 minutes. Add the pasta to the onion-carrot mixture. In a large mixing bowl, stir together the soup, milk, green onions, and dillweed. Stir in the pasta-vegetable mixture. Fold in the peas and tuna. Spoon the mixture into a 1½-quart casserole. Bake, covered, for 20 minutes. Meanwhile, in a small mixing bowl, stir together the crackers and Parmesan. Sprinkle over the tuna mixture and continue to bake, uncovered, for 10 minutes more, or until heated through.

Makes 6 servings

Nutritional information per serving

Calories	285	Cal. from Fat (%)	8.4	Sodium (g)	420
Fat (g)	2.6	Saturated Fat (g)	0.8	Cholesterol (mg)	19
Protein (g)	20.2	Carbohydrate (g)	44		

Ziti Zucchini

The combination of the zucchini with the prosciutto gives this dish so much flavor, you don't need a sauce. If you can't find prosciutto, Canadian bacon can be substituted. As the Italians would say, *magnifico*!

4 cups thinly sliced zucchini
2 ounces prosciutto, cut into
  small pieces
1 bunch green onions
  (scallions), sliced
1 tablespoon minced garlic
½ cup minced parsley

1 (16-ounce) package ziti
  (tubular) pasta
¼ cup grated Parmesan
  cheese
½ teaspoon pepper
Salt to taste

In a large skillet coated with nonstick cooking spray, cook the zucchini, prosciutto, green onion, garlic, and parsley over medium heat, covered, for about 10 minutes, or until the zucchini is tender. Meanwhile, prepare the pasta according to package directions, omitting any oil and salt. Drain and add to the cooked zucchini. Add the Parmesan, pepper, and salt, tossing well.

Makes 6 to 8 servings

Nutritional information per serving

Calories	257	Cal. from Fat (%)	8.1	Sodium (g)	157
Fat (g)	2.3	Saturated Fat (g)	0.8	Cholesterol (mg)	5
Protein (g)	11.1	Carbohydrate (g)	48		

Simply Spinach and Pasta

You can substitute two (10-ounce) packages frozen spinach and defrost the spinach before cooking (drain any water), but this is one time I think fresh spinach is noticeably better.

2 tablespoons minced garlic
2 cups chopped onion
1 pound mushrooms, sliced
1 cup coarsely chopped
  Roma (plum) tomatoes
1 large bunch fresh spinach
  (16 ounces)

Salt and pepper to taste
⅓ cup grated fat-free
  Parmesan cheese
1 tablespoon dried oregano
1 (16-ounce) package ziti
  pasta

Heat a large pot coated with nonstick cooking spray over medium-high heat and cook the garlic, onion, and mushrooms until the vegetables are tender, about 5 minutes. Add the tomatoes and spinach and continue cooking just until the spinach wilts and the tomatoes are heated, about 5 minutes. Add the Parmesan, oregano, and salt and pepper. Meanwhile, cook the pasta according to package directions, omitting any oil and salt. Drain and toss with the spinach mixture.

Makes 6 to 8 servings

Nutritional information per serving

Calories	276	Cal. from Fat (%)	5.5	Sodium (g)	96
Fat (g)	1.7	Saturated Fat (g)	0.2	Cholesterol (mg)	0
Protein (g)	11.7	Carbohydrate (g)	54.1		

Artichoke and Mushroom Fettuccine ♥

The paprika gives the sauce a slight red color and enhances the flavor. Artichokes and mushrooms are such a natural combo, as you will see in this easy dish.

2 tablespoons light stick margarine
½ pound mushrooms, sliced
½ teaspoon minced garlic
2 tablespoons all-purpose flour
1 (14½-ounce) can fat-free chicken broth
1 tablespoon lemon juice

1 teaspoon paprika
Salt and pepper to taste
2 (14-ounce) cans quartered artichoke hearts, drained
1 (8-ounce) package fettuccine pasta
¼ cup grated Parmesan cheese

In a large skillet coated with nonstick cooking spray, melt the margarine and sauté the mushrooms and garlic until tender, about 3 to 5 minutes. Stir in the flour. Gradually add the chicken broth, stirring until the sauce is smooth. Stir in the lemon juice, paprika, salt and pepper, and artichoke hearts and cook until well heated, about 5 minutes. Meanwhile, prepare the pasta according to package directions, omitting any oil and salt. Drain and add to the artichoke sauce with the Parmesan, tossing to mix well.

Makes 4 servings

Nutritional information per serving

Calories	368	Cal. from Fat (%)	17.2	Sodium (g)	811
Fat (g)	7	Saturated Fat (g)	1.9	Cholesterol (mg)	4
Protein (g)	16	Carbohydrate (g)	62.8		

Creamy Tomato Pasta

This dish has a light tomato sauce with a hint of cheese. If you like, you can place the pasta and sauce in a casserole dish, sprinkle with part-skim mozzarella cheese, and bake at 350° F for several minutes, or until the cheese is melted.

1 (28-ounce) can no-salt-added stewed tomatoes, with their juices
1 (28-ounce) can no-salt-added whole tomatoes, drained and chopped
3 tablespoons no-salt-added tomato paste
1 teaspoon minced garlic
1 tablespoon dried oregano
2 teaspoons dried thyme
Salt and pepper to taste

1 (12-ounce) can evaporated skimmed milk
¼ cup dry white wine
1 cup nonfat sour cream
1 cup grated fat-free Parmesan cheese
6 ounces prosciutto, chopped
1 tablespoon dried basil
1 (16-ounce) package fettuccine pasta

In a large pot, combine the stewed tomatoes, chopped tomatoes, tomato paste, garlic, oregano, thyme, and salt and pepper. Bring to a boil, reduce the heat, and simmer, uncovered, over medium heat for 10 minutes. Stir in the evaporated milk and wine. Simmer, stirring occasionally, for 20 minutes. Stir in the sour cream, Parmesan, prosciutto, and basil; simmer 5 minutes more. Do not boil. Meanwhile, cook the pasta according to package directions, omitting any oil and salt. Drain well. Pour the tomato mixture over the hot pasta, tossing until coated.

Makes 8 to 10 servings

Nutritional information per serving

Calories	304	Cal. from Fat (%)	5.8	Sodium (g)	636
Fat (g)	2	Saturated Fat (g)	0.5	Cholesterol (mg)	13
Protein (g)	15.9	Carbohydrate (g)	51.4		

SOUTHWESTERN
DISHES

Chicken Salad Olé

This Southwestern chicken salad is great for a hot summer day. Garnish it with the remaining red onion and serve with chips, and you'll have a delightful meal.

4 cups chopped cooked
    chicken breasts
½ cup shredded reduced-fat
    Cheddar cheese
1 (15-ounce) can black
    beans, drained and rinsed
½ cup chopped red onion
½ cup chopped green bell
    pepper
¼ cup light mayonnaise

⅔ cup nonfat sour cream
1 teaspoon chili powder
½ teaspoon ground cumin
¼ teaspoon dried basil
Salt and pepper to taste
Shredded lettuce
2 medium tomatoes,
    chopped
Low-fat tortilla chips
    (optional)

In a large bowl, combine the chicken, Cheddar, black beans, onion, and green pepper. Mix together the mayonnaise, sour cream, chili powder, cumin, basil, and salt and pepper in a small bowl. Stir into the chicken mixture until well coated. Serve, or cover and refrigerate. Serve on a bed of shredded lettuce topped with the chopped tomato and chips on the side, if desired.

Makes 6 servings

Nutritional information per serving

Calories	330	Cal. from Fat (%)	25.2	Sodium (g)	393
Fat (g)	9.2	Saturated Fat (g)	3.1	Cholesterol (mg)	94
Protein (g)	37.4	Carbohydrate (g)	21.6		

Southwestern Chicken and Black Bean Salad

The well-seasoned chicken makes this salad special. If you're not a cilantro fan, don't skip this recipe; just leave out the cilantro or reduce the amount.

2 teaspoons ground cumin
2 teaspoons chili powder
$\frac{1}{4}$ teaspoon cayenne pepper
2 pounds skinless, boneless chicken breasts, cut into $\frac{1}{2}$-inch strips
2 cups fresh orange sections (about 2 oranges)
1 cup shredded reduced-fat Monterey Jack cheese (optional)
$\frac{1}{2}$ cup chopped red onion

1 (15-ounce) can black beans, drained and rinsed
$\frac{1}{3}$ cup chopped fresh cilantro
$\frac{1}{3}$ cup lime juice
$\frac{1}{4}$ cup orange juice
1 tablespoon canola oil
Salt and pepper to taste
$\frac{1}{2}$ teaspoon minced garlic
1 head lettuce, torn into pieces

Combine the cumin, chili powder, and cayenne in a large zip-top plastic bag. Add the chicken, seal the bag, and shake to coat the chicken with the seasoning mixture. In a skillet coated with nonstick cooking spray, cook the chicken over medium heat until done, about 10 minutes; let cool. Spoon the chicken into a large bowl and add the orange sections, Monterey Jack, onions, black beans, and cilantro, mixing gently but thoroughly. In another bowl, mix the lime juice, orange juice, oil, salt and pepper, and garlic. Pour over the chicken mixture, tossing gently to coat. Serve over the lettuce on a serving platter.

Makes 6 servings

Nutritional information per serving

Calories	322	Cal. from Fat (%)	19.9	Sodium (g)	216
Fat (g)	7.1	Saturated Fat (g)	1.4	Cholesterol (mg)	93
Protein (g)	40	Carbohydrate (g)	24.4		

Rice Taco Salad

Everyone always enjoys tacos, so this salad will appeal to all. It is great even at room temperature.

1 pound ground sirloin
½ cup finely chopped onion
1 garlic clove, minced
½ teaspoon ground cumin
Salt and pepper to taste
3 cups cooked rice
½ head lettuce, shredded

2 tomatoes, chopped
½ cup shredded reduced-fat Cheddar cheese
¼ cup nonfat sour cream
Picante sauce (optional)
Low-fat tortilla chips (optional)

In a large skillet coated with nonstick cooking spray, cook the meat, onion, and garlic over medium heat, stirring to crumble, about 5 to 7 minutes, or until the meat is done. Drain any excess fat. Add the cumin, salt and pepper, and rice. Remove from the heat and let cool. In a large bowl, combine the lettuce, tomatoes, Cheddar, and rice mixture. Add the sour cream; toss lightly. Serve immediately with the picante sauce and tortilla chips, if desired.

Makes 6 servings

Nutritional information per serving

Calories	273	Cal. from Fat (%)	25	Sodium (g)	136
Fat (g)	7.6	Saturated Fat (g)	3.4	Cholesterol (mg)	54
Protein (g)	20.8	Carbohydrate (g)	28.5		

Tex-Mex Tuna Salad

Wow! What a presentation for a tuna salad! As a Southwestern fan, I think this is tuna taken to a new level. This would be great served in a hollowed-out tomato, too, for a nice luncheon.

2 (9-ounce) cans solid white tuna in spring water, drained and flaked
½ cup sliced green onions (scallions)
½ cup chopped celery
1 cup frozen corn, thawed
1 (15-ounce) can black beans, drained and rinsed

½ cup picante sauce
½ cup nonfat sour cream
1 teaspoon ground cumin
Shredded lettuce
Low-fat tortilla chips (optional)

Combine the tuna, green onions, and celery in a medium bowl. Combine the corn, black beans, picante sauce, sour cream, and cumin; mix well. Pour over the tuna mixture; toss lightly. To serve, line individual plates with shredded lettuce and top with the tuna mixture. Surround with tortilla chips, if desired.

Makes 4 servings

Nutritional information per serving

Calories	317	Cal. from Fat (%)	9.5	Sodium (g)	842
Fat (g)	3.3	Saturated Fat (g)	0.8	Cholesterol (mg)	47
Protein (g)	35.9	Carbohydrate (g)	34.4		

Salsa Pasta Salad

If you like salsa, try this pasta salad with its zingy dressing. To make it more substantial, you can add grilled chicken or shrimp.

1 bunch green onions
(scallions), sliced
1 teaspoon minced garlic
1 (28-ounce) can no-salt-
added whole tomatoes,
drained and chopped
1½ tablespoons finely
chopped jalapeño pepper

¼ cup chopped fresh
cilantro
1 teaspoon dried oregano
¼ teaspoon ground cumin
1 (8-ounce) package ziti
(tubular) pasta
1 (15-ounce) can black
beans, drained and rinsed

In a bowl, combine the green onions, garlic, tomatoes, jalapeño, cilantro, oregano, and cumin. Cook the pasta according to the package directions, omitting any oil and salt. Drain and rinse. Let cool and toss with the tomato mixture and the black beans. Serve, or cover and refrigerate.

Makes 4 servings

Nutritional information per serving

Calories	349	Cal. from Fat (%)	4.1	Sodium (g)	189
Fat (g)	1.6	Saturated Fat (g)	0.3	Cholesterol (mg)	0
Protein (g)	15.6	Carbohydrate (g)	68.3		

Southwestern Shrimp and Angel Hair

This wonderful pasta dish will quickly attract you because of the color and taste.

2 tablespoons olive oil
1 red bell pepper, seeded and coarsely chopped
1 teaspoon minced garlic
1 bunch green onions (scallions), chopped
1 small onion, chopped
2 pounds medium shrimp, peeled
3 tablespoons lemon juice

1 (4-ounce) can chopped ripe black olives, drained
1 (11-ounce) can white shoe peg corn, drained
1 tablespoon chili powder
¼ teaspoon ground cumin
Dash of cayenne
1 (12-ounce) package angel hair (capellini) pasta

Heat the oil in a large skillet coated with nonstick cooking spray over medium heat and sauté the red pepper, garlic, green onions, and onion until tender, about 5 minutes. Add the shrimp and cook, stirring, until they begin to turn pink, about 3 minutes. Add the lemon juice, olives, corn, chili powder, cumin, and cayenne, stirring until heated. Meanwhile, cook the pasta according to the package directions, omitting any oil and salt. Drain the pasta and add to the shrimp mixture, tossing to mix well.

Makes 8 servings

Nutritional information per serving

Calories	291	Cal. from Fat (%)	17.8	Sodium (g)	261
Fat (g)	5.8	Saturated Fat (g)	0.8	Cholesterol (mg)	81
Protein (g)	15.9	Carbohydrate (g)	44.8		

Beef and Salsa Fajitas

This marinade is so good that you'll enjoy these fajitas equally well inside or on the grill. The meat takes eight hours to marinate, so plan ahead.

⅔ cup lime juice
1 cup light beer
2 tablespoons minced fresh
  cilantro
2 teaspoons dried oregano
¼ teaspoon crushed red
  pepper flakes
1 teaspoon dried cumin
1 garlic clove, minced
1 green bell pepper, seeded
  and cut into 1-inch squares
1 red bell pepper, seeded
  and cut into 1-inch squares
2 pounds lean, boneless, top
  round steak

1 small red onion, cut into
  rings
1½ cups diced tomato
⅔ cup chopped green onions
  (scallions)
¼ cup chopped fresh
  cilantro
3 tablespoons red wine
  vinegar
1 tablespoon chopped
  jalapeño pepper
8 (8-inch) flour tortillas

Combine the lime juice, beer, cilantro, oregano, red pepper flakes, cumin, garlic, green pepper, and red pepper in a large heavy-duty zip-top plastic bag; seal the bag and shake well. Place the steak and red onion in the bag and marinate in the refrigerator for 8 hours. In a bowl, combine the tomato, green onions, cilantro, vinegar, and jalapeño. Cover and chill. Remove the steak and vegetables from the marinade, reserving the marinade. Broil or grill the steak, basting occasionally with the marinade, for 5 to 6 minutes on each side, or until desired doneness is reached. Cut the steak diagonally across the grain into ¼-inch wide slices. In a skillet, sauté the marinated onion and green and red peppers until tender, about 5 minutes. Meanwhile, heat the tortillas. Divide the steak and vegetables among the tortillas. Top each with 3 tablespoons of the tomato salsa mixture, roll up the tortillas, and serve.

Makes 4 servings

Nutritional information per serving

Calories	687	Cal. from Fat (%)	23.6	Sodium (g)	614
Fat (g)	18	Saturated Fat (g)	5.1	Cholesterol (mg)	130
Protein (g)	55.3	Carbohydrate (g)	71.6		

Crawfish Enchiladas

Here is a fabulous new combination for you—a white creamy sauce with crawfish and a Southwestern flair! Small shrimp can be used instead of crawfish—just don't skip the recipe.

½ cup chopped onion
1 tablespoon chopped
  Anaheim pepper
½ cup chopped green bell
  pepper
½ teaspoon minced garlic
Salt and pepper to taste
Dash of cayenne pepper
½ teaspoon dried oregano
1 (12-ounce) can evaporated
  skimmed milk

1 cup nonfat sour cream
1 pound crawfish tails,
  rinsed and drained
½ teaspoon chili powder
1 bunch green onions
  (scallions), chopped
8 (10-inch) flour tortillas
1 cup shredded reduced-fat
  Monterey Jack cheese

Preheat the oven to 350° F. In a pot coated with nonstick cooking spray, sauté the onion, Anaheim pepper, green pepper, garlic, salt and pepper, cayenne, and oregano until the vegetables are tender, about 5 minutes. Add the evaporated milk and simmer for 10 minutes. Add the sour cream but do not boil, stirring until well mixed. Remove from the heat. In another pan coated with nonstick cooking spray, sauté the crawfish tails, chili powder, and green onions until tender, about 5 minutes. Add the crawfish mixture to the creamed mixture. Spoon the crawfish and sauce (about ½ cup) into each tortilla and roll. Place, seam side down, in a 3-quart oblong baking dish coated with nonstick cooking spray. Pour the remainder of the sauce over the stuffed tortillas. Sprinkle with the Monterey Jack. Bake for 5 minutes, or until the cheese is melted.

Makes 8 large enchiladas

Nutritional information per serving

Calories	436	Cal. from Fat (%)	20.2	Sodium (g)	668
Fat (g)	9.8	Saturated Fat (g)	3.1	Cholesterol (mg)	94
Protein (g)	25.8	Carbohydrate (g)	59.3		

Southwestern Fish

You can use this topping recipe over chicken as well. The presentation is very impressive, one that your guests will remember.

2 pounds fish fillets (orange
   roughy, trout, or other
   mild fish)
2 tablespoons lime juice
1 teaspoon minced garlic
1 onion, chopped
1 (4½-ounce) can chopped
   green chilies, drained
½ teaspoon dried cumin

2 teaspoons chili powder
1 (15-ounce) can black
   beans, drained and rinsed
1 cup frozen corn, thawed
1 cup chopped Roma (plum)
   tomatoes
¼ cup chopped fresh
   cilantro

Preheat the oven to 350°F. Lay the fish fillets in a 13 × 9 × 2-inch oblong pan coated with nonstick cooking spray. Sprinkle with the lime juice. In a large pan coated with nonstick cooking spray, sauté the garlic and onion over medium heat until tender, about 3 minutes. Add the green chilies, cumin, chili powder, black beans, corn, and tomatoes, stirring until well heated, about 5 minutes. Add the cilantro. Spoon the sauce over the fish. Bake, covered, for 25 minutes, or until the fish flakes easily when tested with a fork.

Makes 8 to 10 servings

Nutritional information per serving

Calories	200	Cal. from Fat (%)	28.9	Sodium (g)	274
Fat (g)	6.4	Saturated Fat (g)	1.1	Cholesterol (mg)	52
Protein (g)	22.2	Carbohydrate (g)	13.5		

Spicy Chicken Enchiladas

The spicy red sauce goes really well with the chicken filling. You can use black beans instead of pintos if you like.

1½ pounds skinless, boneless chicken breasts, cut into bite-size pieces
1 cup chopped red onion
1 large green bell pepper, seeded and chopped
2 tablespoons chopped fresh cilantro
1 tablespoon chili powder
1 (16-ounce) can pinto beans, drained and rinsed

1 (14½-ounce) can diced tomatoes and green chilies, drained
1 (8-ounce) can no-salt-added tomato sauce
¼ teaspoon pepper
1 cup shredded reduced-fat Monterey Jack cheese
12 (8-inch) flour tortillas

Preheat the oven to 350° F. Place the chicken in a large skillet coated with nonstick cooking spray and sauté over medium-high heat until lightly browned, about 5 minutes. Add the onion, green pepper, and cilantro and sauté 3 minutes more, or until the chicken is done. Remove from the heat. Add the chili powder and beans; stir. In a bowl, combine the tomatoes and green chilies, tomato sauce, and pepper; stir. Spoon ⅓ cup of the tomato mixture into a 3-quart oblong baking dish coated with nonstick cooking spray. Set the remaining tomato mixture aside. Divide the chicken mixture and Monterey Jack evenly down the center of each tortilla. Roll the tortillas tightly and place, seam side down, in the baking dish. Pour the remaining tomato mixture over the tortillas. Cover and bake for 30 minutes, or until thoroughly heated.

Makes 12 enchiladas

Nutritional information per serving

Calories	319	Cal. from Fat (%)	21.1	Sodium (g)	568
Fat (g)	7.5	Saturated Fat (g)	2.4	Cholesterol (mg)	41
Protein (g)	22.6	Carbohydrate (g)	40.4		

Crispy Chicken and Bean Burritos ♥

Those who like a deluxe burrito that tastes like it's an absolute no-no will enjoy this dish. It does have a few steps, but it's worth the effort. For a bean burrito, just leave out the chicken. Also, you can serve with salsa on the side.

2 pounds skinless, boneless chicken breasts, cut into bite-size pieces
1 onion, chopped
1 green bell pepper, seeded and chopped
1 teaspoon minced garlic
1 (4-ounce) can diced green chilies, drained
2 (15-ounce) cans pinto beans, drained and rinsed, mashed

1 (8-ounce) package fat-free cream cheese
¼ cup light mayonnaise
12 (8-inch) flour tortillas
1 cup chopped green onions (scallions)
1 cup salsa
1 (15-ounce) can enchilada sauce
1 cup shredded reduced-fat Monterey Jack cheese

Preheat the oven to 350° F. In a large skillet coated with nonstick cooking spray, cook the chicken until lightly browned, about 5 minutes. Add the onion, green pepper, and garlic and sauté until the chicken is done and the vegetables are tender, about 5 to 7 minutes. Add the green chilies and pinto beans, stirring until thoroughly heated. In a small bowl, combine the cream cheese and mayonnaise; mix well. Soften the tortillas in the microwave for 30 seconds. Spoon about ¼ cup of the chicken-bean mixture down one side of each tortilla. Top each tortilla evenly with the cream cheese mixture, green onions, and salsa. Roll up the tortillas and arrange seam side down in a baking dish. Cover with the enchilada sauce and bake, covered, for 25 minutes. Uncover and sprinkle with the Monterey Jack and continue baking 10 minutes more or until the cheese is melted.

Makes 12 servings

Nutritional information per serving

Calories	420	Cal. from Fat (%)	22.5	Sodium (g)	987
Fat (g)	10.5	Saturated Fat (g)	2.9	Cholesterol (mg)	57
Protein (g)	30.8	Carbohydrate (g)	49.4		

Mexican Chicken Casserole

This is a super way to use leftover chicken. In fact, the casserole is so good you'll even cook the chicken for it. I'm sure you've seen many Mexican chicken casseroles, but this is one of my favorites. It serves a crowd and can be made ahead.

1 green bell pepper, seeded
  and chopped
1 onion, chopped
2 cups chopped tomatoes
1 (10½-ounce) can reduced-
  fat cream of chicken soup
1 (10½-ounce) can reduced-
  fat cream of mushroom
  soup

⅔ cup picante sauce
1 tablespoon chili powder
12 (6-inch) flour tortillas, cut
  into 1-inch strips
2½ pounds cooked chicken
  breast, cut into pieces
1 cup shredded reduced-fat
  Cheddar cheese

Preheat the oven to 350° F. In a large pot coated with nonstick cooking spray, sauté the green pepper and onion until tender, about 3 to 5 minutes. Remove from the heat and add the tomatoes, cream of chicken soup, cream of mushroom soup, picante sauce, and chili powder, mixing well. Line the bottom of a 3-quart casserole dish coated with nonstick cooking spray with half the tortilla strips. Top with half the chicken and half the soup mixture. Repeat the layers and sprinkle the top with the Cheddar. Bake, uncovered, for 35 to 45 minutes, or until the casserole is bubbly.

Makes 6 to 8 servings

Nutritional information per serving

Calories	523	Cal. from Fat (%)	23.5	Sodium (g)	955
Fat (g)	13.6	Saturated Fat (g)	4.7	Cholesterol (mg)	139
Protein (g)	53.8	Carbohydrate (g)	42.6		

Tamale Pie ♥

My brother-in-law thought this tasted like hot tamales. This dish is great for a crowd, and people of all ages will clean their plates.

2 pounds ground sirloin
1 onion, chopped
1 teaspoon minced garlic
1 (8-ounce) can no-salt-added tomato sauce
1 (16-ounce) jar thick and chunky salsa
1 teaspoon dried cumin

1 teaspoon chili powder
1 (15-ounce) can creamed-style corn
6 (8-inch) flour tortillas, cut into 1-inch strips
½ cup shredded reduced-fat Cheddar cheese

Preheat the oven to 350° F. In a large skillet coated with nonstick cooking spray, cook the meat, onion, and garlic, about 8 minutes, or until the meat is done. Drain any excess grease. Add the tomato sauce, salsa, cumin, chili powder, and corn. Mix well. Coat a 13 × 9 × 2-inch baking pan with nonstick cooking spray and layer the mixture with the tortilla strips, starting with a fourth of the meat mixture and topping with a third of the tortilla strips. Continue layering, ending with the meat mixture. Cover and bake for 35 to 40 minutes, or until thoroughly heated. Sprinkle with the Cheddar and continue cooking another 5 minutes.

Makes 10 to 12 servings

Nutritional information per serving

Calories	212	Cal. from Fat (%)	24.6	Sodium (g)	525
Fat (g)	5.8	Saturated Fat (g)	2.2	Cholesterol (mg)	47
Protein (g)	18.6	Carbohydrate (g)	20.7		

Speedy Southwest Pasta Casserole

A great family layered dish which includes all the basics: pasta, meat sauce, and cheese.

2 pounds ground sirloin
2 onions, chopped
2 green bell peppers, seeded and chopped
1 tablespoon minced garlic
2 tablespoons chili powder
1 teaspoon ground cumin
1 teaspoon dried oregano
Salt and pepper to taste
1 (15-ounce) can no-salt-added tomato sauce

1 (14½-ounce) can no-salt-added whole tomatoes, crushed, with their juices
1 (16-ounce) package angel hair (capellini) pasta
1 cup skim milk
2 large eggs
1 cup shredded reduced-fat Cheddar cheese

Preheat the oven to 425° F. In a large skillet, cook the meat, onions, green pepper, and garlic over medium heat about 5 to 7 minutes, or until the meat is done. Drain any excess grease. Add the chili powder, cumin, oregano, salt and pepper, tomato sauce, and crushed tomatoes. Cook for 5 minutes longer. Meanwhile, cook the pasta according to package directions, omitting any oil and salt. Drain and set aside. In a bowl, mix the milk and eggs together. Combine with the pasta and place the pasta in a 3-quart oblong baking dish coated with nonstick cooking spray. Spread the meat mixture on top. Bake, uncovered, for 30 minutes. Sprinkle with the Cheddar and bake 5 minutes longer, or until the cheese is melted.

Makes 10 to 12 servings

Nutritional information per serving

Calories	323	Cal. from Fat (%)	20.2	Sodium (g)	157
Fat (g)	7.2	Saturated Fat (g)	3	Cholesterol (mg)	86
Protein (g)	25.3	Carbohydrate (g)	37.8		

Crispy Southwestern Lasagne

The corn tortillas combined with all these great ingredients make this crispy lasagne extremely popular.

1 pound ground sirloin
1 (14½-ounce) can no-salt-added diced tomatoes, with their juices
1 (4-ounce) can diced green chilies, drained
2 teaspoons chili powder
1½ teaspoons ground cumin
1 teaspoon minced garlic
Salt and pepper to taste

2 large egg whites
2 cups nonfat cottage cheese
14 (6-inch) corn tortillas, cut in quarters
1 (17-ounce) can whole-kernel corn, drained
1 (8-ounce) package reduced-fat Monterey Jack cheese, shredded

Preheat the oven to 350° F. In a large skillet coated with nonstick cooking spray, cook the meat until done, about 5 minutes. Drain any excess grease. Add the tomatoes, green chilies, chili powder, cumin, garlic, and salt and pepper; set aside. In a small bowl, combine the egg whites and cottage cheese; set aside. Coat a 13 × 9 × 2-inch baking dish with nonstick cooking spray. Cover the bottom of the baking dish with 6 corn tortillas (cut in quarters). Place a layer of all the corn, half the meat mixture, a third of the Monterey Jack, 4 tortillas (cut in quarters), then all the cottage cheese mixture, the remaining half of the meat mixture, and the remaining 4 tortillas and top with the remaining cheese. Bake, uncovered, for 30 minutes.

Makes 8 servings

Nutritional information per serving

Calories	354	Cal. from Fat (%) 27.1	Sodium (g)	722
Fat (g)	10.7	Saturated Fat (g) 5.4	Cholesterol (mg)	60
Protein (g)	32.7	Carbohydrate (g) 34.5		

Enchilada Casserole

This great Mexican casserole can be put together in the morning and baked that night for dinner. If you refrigerate the casserole in a glass baking dish, place it in a cold oven and bake it at 350° F for 15 minutes longer than the recipe says.

1 pound ground sirloin	1 (4-ounce) can diced green
2 garlic cloves, minced	chilies, drained
½ cup chopped onion	10 (6-inch) flour tortillas
Salt and pepper to taste	1½ cups shredded reduced-
1 teaspoon chili powder	fat Monterey Jack cheese
2 tomatoes, chopped	1 cup nonfat sour cream
1 (10-ounce) can enchilada	
sauce	

Preheat the oven to 350° F. In large skillet coated with nonstick cooking spray, cook the meat with the garlic, onion, salt, pepper, and chili powder until the meat is browned, about 7 minutes. Drain any excess grease. Add the tomatoes, enchilada sauce, and green chilies. Mix well. Cover and simmer for 10 minutes. Cut the tortillas into quarters. Coat a 13 × 9 × 2-inch baking dish coated with nonstick cooking spray and cover the bottom with half the tortilla quarters, overlapping slightly. Spoon half of the meat mixture over the tortillas. Sprinkle with half the Monterey Jack. Arrange the remaining tortilla quarters over the cheese, overlapping slightly. Spread with the sour cream. Spoon the remaining meat mixture over the sour cream. Sprinkle with the remaining cheese. Bake, covered, for 45 minutes. Uncover and bake for 5 minutes longer, or until the cheese is melted.

Makes 8 servings

Nutritional information per serving

Calories	314	Cal. from Fat (%) 30.6		Sodium (g)	539
Fat (g)	10.7	Saturated Fat (g) 4.4		Cholesterol (mg)	53
Protein (g)	21.3	Carbohydrate (g) 32.3			

Southwestern Pot Roast

Thumbs up for this one! A pot roast is always delicious, but with a Southwestern flair, you have a new favorite for family meals.

4 pounds bottom round
  roast, trimmed
Salt and pepper to taste
1 cup chopped red onion
1 teaspoon minced garlic
1 green bell pepper, seeded
  and chopped
1 cup canned beef broth

3 tablespoons chili powder
¼ teaspoon cayenne pepper
1 (16-ounce) can red kidney
  beans, drained and rinsed
4 ears fresh or frozen corn,
  thawed, cut into 4-inch
  pieces

Preheat the oven to 400° F. Season the roast with salt and pepper and place in a large roasting pan coated with nonstick cooking spray. Bake for 10 minutes, then turn over and bake for another 10 minutes, to brown on both sides. Add the onion, garlic, green pepper, beef broth, chili powder, and cayenne. Spoon the sauce over the roast, cover, and continue baking for 2½ hours, turning the roast every 30 minutes. Add the kidney beans and corn and continue cooking for 30 minutes longer, or until the roast is very tender. Slice the roast and serve with the beans and corn.

Makes 8 servings

Nutritional information per serving

Calories	419	Cal. from Fat (%)	26.5	Sodium (g)	438
Fat (g)	12.3	Saturated Fat (g)	3.9	Cholesterol (mg)	130
Protein (g)	53.8	Carbohydrate (g)	23		

Pork Southwestern Style

It's not very often my husband raves about a recipe, but he thought this one was a winner. The cumin gives it that subtle Southwestern flavor, and the salsa, corn, and red onion make it a very colorful dish.

1¼ pounds pork tenderloin,
 cut into ¾-inch slices
1½ teaspoons ground cumin
1 teaspoon minced garlic
1 red onion, cut into thin
 wedges
1 (14½-ounce) can no-salt-
 added whole tomatoes

¾ cup salsa
1 (10-ounce) package frozen
 corn
2 tablespoons chopped fresh
 cilantro
3 cups cooked rice

In a large skillet coated with nonstick cooking spray, brown the pork on each side for 3 minutes over medium heat. Sprinkle on all sides with the cumin. Add the garlic and onion and continue cooking for 3 to 5 minutes. Add the tomatoes and salsa, bring to a boil, and cook for 20 minutes. Add the corn and continue cooking another 10 minutes, or until the pork is tender. Sprinkle with the cilantro and serve over the rice.

Makes 4 servings

Nutritional information per serving

Calories	440	Cal. from Fat (%)	14.4	Sodium (g)	409
Fat (g)	7	Saturated Fat (g)	2.4	Cholesterol (mg)	84
Protein (g)	36.1	Carbohydrate (g)	57		

MEATLESS
MAIN DISHES

Vegetable Medley Lasagne

It's always nice to have some lasagne recipes on hand so you can serve up a dish that will make both vegetarians and any hearty eaters happy.

2 tablespoons olive oil
1 onion, chopped
2 cloves garlic, minced
1 tablespoon dried basil
1 tablespoon dried
 rosemary
⅓ cup dry red wine

3 (14½-ounce) cans no-salt-
 added whole tomatoes,
 chopped, with their juices
1 (8-ounce) package lasagne
 noodles
Vegetable Filling (recipe
 follows)

Preheat the oven to 375° F. In a large pan, heat the oil over medium heat and sauté the onion and garlic until tender, about 5 minutes. Add the basil, rosemary, wine, and tomatoes with their juice. Simmer 20 to 30 minutes, until slightly thickened. Meanwhile, cook the lasagne noodles according to the package directions, omitting any oil and salt. Drain and rinse. Coat a large rectangular baking dish with nonstick cooking spray. Spread a third of the sauce on the bottom. Add a layer of half the noodles and a layer of half the Vegetable Filling. Repeat the layers ending with the last third of the sauce. Cover and bake for 20 minutes. Uncover and bake for 10 more minutes, or until hot and bubbly. Serve immediately.

Makes 8 to 10 servings

Vegetable Filling

1 cup broccoli florets
1 cup chopped peeled
 carrots
½ pound mushrooms, sliced
1 (15-ounce) container low-
 fat ricotta cheese

½ cup grated Parmesan
 cheese
¼ cup dry white wine
¾ cup nonfat sour cream
1 tablespoon dried basil

Combine the broccoli, carrots, and mushrooms in a microwaveproof bowl with a little water. Cover and cook in the microwave until tender, 4 to 7 minutes. Drain and set aside to cool. In a large bowl, combine the ricotta, Parmesan, wine, sour cream, and basil. Carefully mix in the cooked vegetables.

Calories	216	Cal. from Fat (%) 24.3		Sodium (g)	183
Fat (g)	5.8	Saturated Fat (g) 2.2		Cholesterol (mg)	23
Protein (g)	12.7	Carbohydrate (g) 26.8			

Spinach Roll-Ups ♥

You can prepare these tasty, attractive roll-ups ahead of time and bake before serving. Think of this recipe as rolled-up lasagne. You can even add canned mushrooms to the tomato sauce for extra flair.

12 lasagne noodles
2 large egg whites
2 (10-ounce) packages frozen chopped spinach, thawed and squeezed dry
1 cup low-fat ricotta cheese
1/4 cup grated Parmesan cheese
1/4 teaspoon pepper
1/8 teaspoon ground nutmeg

1 teaspoon minced garlic, divided
1 (14 1/2-ounce) can no-salt-added tomatoes, chopped with their juices
1 tablespoon all-purpose flour
1 teaspoon dried basil
1 teaspoon dried oregano

Preheat the oven to 400° F. Cook the lasagne noodles according to package directions, omitting any oil and salt. Drain, rinse, and set aside. In a large bowl, mix together the egg whites, spinach, ricotta, Parmesan, pepper, nutmeg, and 1/2 teaspoon of the garlic. Lay a noodle flat on a work surface. Spread about 1/4 cup of the filling over the noodle and roll it up. Place the lasagna roll seam side down in a baking pan coated with nonstick cooking spray. Repeat with the remaining noodles and filling. In a medium bowl, combine the tomatoes, flour, basil, oregano, and the remaining garlic. Pour the sauce over the lasagne rolls and bake, uncovered, for 25 minutes, or until bubbly.

Makes 6 servings

Calories	246	Cal. from Fat (%) 11.6		Sodium (g)	211
Fat (g)	3.2	Saturated Fat (g) 1.7		Cholesterol (mg)	18
Protein (g)	16.2	Carbohydrate (g) 39.8			

Spinach Manicotti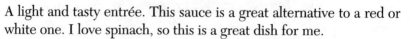

A light and tasty entrée. This sauce is a great alternative to a red or white one. I love spinach, so this is a great dish for me.

1 (8-ounce) package
   manicotti shells
1 (10-ounce) package frozen
   chopped spinach
1 (16-ounce) container low-
   fat ricotta cheese
1 large egg white, beaten
Salt and pepper to taste

Dash of ground nutmeg
½ cup shredded part-skim
   mozzarella cheese
1 tablespoon olive oil
1 large tomato, chopped
½ teaspoon minced garlic
1 onion, chopped

Preheat the oven to 350° F. Cook the manicotti shells according to package directions, omitting any oil and salt. Drain and set aside. Meanwhile, cook the spinach according to package directions; drain well, squeezing out any excess liquid. In a bowl, combine the spinach with the ricotta, egg white, salt and pepper, nutmeg, and mozzarella. Stuff the cooked shells with the spinach-cheese mixture and place in a 2-quart oblong baking dish coated with nonstick cooking spray. In a small pan coated with nonstick cooking spray, heat the oil over medium heat and sauté the tomato, garlic, and onion until tender, about 5 minutes. Pour over the manicotti, cover, and bake for 30 minutes.

Makes 8 servings

Nutritional information per serving

Calories	198	Cal. from Fat (%)	24	Sodium (g)	162
Fat (g)	4.6	Saturated Fat (g)	2.4	Cholesterol (mg)	27
Protein (g)	14.8	Carbohydrate (g)	24.7		

Layered Pasta and Spinach Surprise ♥

The creamy, cheesy spinach combined with the pasta and picante sauce makes this casserole an exciting blend of Italian and Tex-Mex flavors.

1 (8-ounce) package mostaccioli or other tubular pasta
2 (10-ounce) packages frozen chopped spinach, thawed and squeezed dry
12 ounces fat-free cream cheese, softened
¾ cup skim milk
1 teaspoon dried oregano
2 teaspoons minced garlic

2 cups picante sauce
1 (8-ounce) can no-salt-added tomato sauce
2 teaspoons chili powder
1½ teaspoons ground cumin
½ cup chopped green onions (scallions)
1 (8-ounce) package reduced-fat Monterey Jack cheese, shredded

Preheat the oven to 350° F. Cook the pasta according to package directions, omitting any oil and salt. Drain, rinse, and set aside. In a bowl, combine the spinach, cream cheese, milk, oregano, and garlic, blending well with a fork. In a large saucepan, mix the picante sauce, tomato sauce, chili powder, and cumin. Bring to a boil, reduce the heat, and cook 5 minutes longer. Combine the pasta with the sauce, mixing well. Place half the pasta mixture in a 13 × 9 × 2-inch baking dish coated with nonstick cooking spray. Carefully spread all the spinach-cheese mixture over the pasta and cover with the remaining pasta. Cover and bake for 30 minutes. Sprinkle with the green onions and Monterey Jack and continue baking, uncovered, for several minutes, or until the cheese is melted.

Makes 6 servings

Nutritional information per serving

Calories	383	Cal. from Fat (%)	21.9	Sodium (g)	1324
Fat (g)	9.3	Saturated Fat (g)	5.6	Cholesterol (mg)	34
Protein (g)	26.9	Carbohydrate (g)	49.3		

Mushroom Lasagne

The creamy white sauce combined with the mushrooms and the cheese gives this lasagne a rich flavor. Lasagne is the perfect one-dish meal, and even saying the word makes everyone's eyes light up.

1 (8-ounce) package lasagne noodles
1 pound mushrooms, sliced
1 teaspoon minced garlic
⅓ cup all-purpose flour
2½ cups skim milk
½ cup chopped parsley

1 (15-ounce) container low-fat ricotta cheese
1 large egg white, slightly beaten
1 (8-ounce) package part-skim mozzarella cheese, shredded

Preheat the oven to 350° F. Cook the lasagne noodles according to the package directions, omitting any oil and salt. Drain well, rinse, and set aside. In a large pan coated with nonstick cooking spray, sauté the mushrooms and garlic over medium heat, stirring constantly, until tender, about 5 minutes. Reduce the heat to low and add the flour, mixing well. Gradually stir in the milk; cook over medium heat, stirring constantly, until the mixture is thickened and bubbly, about 5 minutes. Add the parsley, stirring well. Spread 1 cup of the mushroom mixture in a 13 × 9 × 2-inch baking dish coated with nonstick cooking spray. Layer a third of the noodles over the mushroom mixture. Mix together the ricotta and egg white. Spread half of the ricotta mixture evenly over the noodles. Sprinkle half the mozzarella over the ricotta. Spread another 1 cup of the mushroom mixture over the mozzarella. Repeat with the noodles, ricotta, and mozzarella, ending with a layer of noodles on top and then the remaining mushroom sauce. Cover with foil and bake for 40 minutes, or until the lasagne is bubbly.

Makes 12 servings

Nutritional information per serving

Calories	188	Cal. from Fat (%) 23.8		Sodium (g)	194
Fat (g)	5	Saturated Fat (g)	3	Cholesterol (mg)	25
Protein (g)	15.6	Carbohydrate (g) 21.1			

Stuffed Pasta Peppers

For this super selection, I prefer to use the red and yellow bell peppers if they are available and affordable.

6 medium bell peppers (green, yellow, and/or red)	1 teaspoon minced garlic
8 ounces small pasta shells	1 tablespoon all-purpose flour
½ cup sliced green onion (scallions)	1 (5-ounce) can evaporated skimmed milk
½ pound mushrooms, sliced	2 tablespoons dry sherry
1 cup thinly sliced zucchini	Salt and pepper to taste
1 cup chopped Roma (plum) tomatoes	⅓ cup grated Parmesan cheese

Trim the tops from the bell peppers and discard the seeds inside. Place in a microwaveproof dish with ½ cup water, cover, and microwave for 4 minutes. Drain and set aside. Prepare the pasta according to the package directions, omitting any oil and salt. Drain and set aside. Preheat the oven to 400° F. In a large skillet coated with nonstick cooking spray, sauté the green onion, mushrooms, zucchini, tomatoes, and garlic over medium heat for 7 to 9 minutes, or until the vegetables are tender. Stir in the flour and gradually add the evaporated milk, stirring until the mixture is thickened. Add the sherry and salt and pepper. Stir in the pasta and Parmesan, mixing until the pasta is thoroughly heated and the cheese is melted. Divide the pasta mixture evenly among the bell peppers and place them standing upright in a baking dish filled with ½ cup water. Cover the dish with foil and bake for 20 minutes.

Makes 6 servings

Nutritional information per serving

Calories	251	Cal. from Fat (%)	9.4	Sodium (g)	123
Fat (g)	2.6	Saturated Fat (g)	1	Cholesterol (mg)	4
Protein (g)	11.5	Carbohydrate (g)	45.7		

Squash, Tomato, and Bow-Tie Pasta ♥

When tomatoes are in season, be sure to remember this simple dish. I like the smaller squash—as they're more tender.

1 (16-ounce) package bow-tie pasta	¼ cup grated Parmesan cheese
2½ pounds yellow summer squash, thinly sliced	Pepper to taste
2 cups chopped tomatoes	1 bunch green onions (scallions), chopped
1 teaspoon dried basil	

Cook the pasta according to package directions, omitting any oil and salt. Drain; set aside. In a large pan coated with nonstick cooking spray, cook the yellow squash and the tomatoes over medium heat, covered, stirring occasionally, until tender, about 10 minutes. Add the basil, Parmesan, pepper, and green onions, mixing thoroughly. Toss the squash mixture with the pasta.

Makes 6 servings

Nutritional information per serving

Calories	363	Cal. from Fat (%)	7.7	Sodium (g)	77
Fat (g)	3.1	Saturated Fat (g)	1	Cholesterol (mg)	3
Protein (g)	14	Carbohydrate (g)	70.8		

Garden Pasta ♥

If you're lucky and industrious enough to have a garden, this colorful pasta is the perfect choice. With all the wonderful vegetables combined with dill, you won't even miss a sauce. I use lots of black pepper, too.

2 tablespoons olive oil	2 cups chopped Roma (plum) tomatoes
1 cup 2-inch slices yellow squash	1 green bell pepper, seeded and cut into strips
1 cup 2-inch slices zucchini	2 teaspoons dried dillweed
8 ounces fresh green beans, ends snapped	Salt and pepper to taste
2 cups 2-inch slices peeled carrots	1 (16-ounce) package penne pasta
1 bunch green onions (scallions), chopped	

In a large skillet coated with nonstick cooking spray, heat the oil over medium-high heat and sauté the yellow squash, zucchini, green beans, carrots, green onions, tomatoes, and green pepper until tender, about 8 minutes. Add the dillweed and salt and pepper. Meanwhile, prepare the pasta according to package directions, omitting any oil and salt. Drain and toss with the vegetable mixture.

Makes 8 servings

Nutritional information per serving

Calories	286	Cal. from Fat (%) 14.9		Sodium (g)	16
Fat (g)	4.7	Saturated Fat (g)	0.7	Cholesterol (mg)	0
Protein (g)	9.2	Carbohydrate (g) 52.5			

Hot Potatoes

This is a very attractive as well as tasty potato dish. It's a spicy one, so get ready!

4 potatoes, peeled and cut into ¼-inch round slices
1¼ teaspoons minced garlic, divided
Salt and pepper to taste
1 tablespoon olive oil

1 (4½-ounce) can chopped green chilies, drained
½ cup minced fresh cilantro
1 large tomato, diced
½ cup shredded reduced-fat Monterey Jack cheese

Preheat the oven to 350° F. Coat a baking sheet and a 9-inch pizza pan with nonstick cooking spray. In a large bowl, combine the sliced potatoes, 1 teaspoon of the garlic, the salt and pepper, and the oil. Mix well. Spread the potato slices in a single layer on the baking sheet. Bake 20 to 25 minutes, or until tender. In a small bowl, combine the green chilies, cilantro, tomato, and the remaining garlic. Set aside. In the pizza pan, arrange the baked sliced potatoes in a spiral pattern, overlapping the slices. Spoon the chili mixture over the potatoes and top with the shredded Monterey Jack. Bake for 5 to 6 minutes, or until the cheese is melted. To serve, cut into wedges.

Makes 4 servings

Nutritional information per serving

Calories	159	Cal. from Fat (%) 25.5		Sodium (g)	477
Fat (g)	4.5	Saturated Fat (g)	1.7	Cholesterol (mg)	7
Protein (g)	5	Carbohydrate (g) 26.4			

Thai Pasta Dish

Here is a quick trip to Bangkok in the kitchen. I've mainstreamed this popular Thai dish, so this is a good time to sample this country's cuisine.

1 (8-ounce) package
  vermicelli pasta
1 cup fresh bean sprouts
½ cup sliced green onions
  (scallions)
1 (7-ounce) jar or can
  pickled or plain whole
  baby corn, drained
2 tablespoons chopped
  peanuts

1 (4-ounce) can mushrooms,
  drained
3 large egg whites
½ teaspoon garlic powder
1 cup bottled pad thai or
  sweet-and-sour stir-fry
  sauce

Cook the pasta according to package directions, omitting any oil and salt. Drain; set aside. In a bowl, toss together the bean sprouts, green onions, corn, and peanuts; set aside. In a saucepan coated with nonstick cooking spray, sauté the mushrooms over medium heat until hot, about 2 minutes. Beat the egg whites slightly with the garlic powder in a small bowl. Pour over the mushrooms. Stir in the bottled sauce, pasta, and vegetable mixture. Continue cooking, tossing gently, until the pasta is heated through and the egg whites are cooked, about 5 to 8 minutes.

Makes 4 to 6 servings

Nutritional information per serving

Calories	242	Cal. from Fat (%)	9.6	Sodium (g)	222
Fat (g)	2.6	Saturated Fat (g)	0.5	Cholesterol (mg)	0
Protein (g)	8.8	Carbohydrate (g)	46.1		

Eggplant and Ziti ♥

This simple eggplant dish with a red sauce is full of big Italian flavors. If you like, sprinkle it with Parmesan cheese.

1 medium eggplant (about 1 pound)	2 (14½-ounce) cans no-salt-added tomatoes, crushed, with their juices
Salt	
1 large onion, chopped	1 teaspoon dried oregano
½ pound mushrooms, sliced	½ teaspoon dried basil
1 teaspoon minced garlic	1 (12-ounce) package ziti pasta

Peel and slice the eggplant into ½-inch round slices. Sprinkle the slices with a bit of salt and let drain in a colander for 30 minutes. Rinse the slices and pat dry. In a large saucepan coated with non-stick cooking spray, sauté the onion, mushrooms, and garlic until tender, about 5 to 7 minutes. Cut the eggplant slices into quarters and add to the pan. Stir in the tomatoes, oregano, and basil. Cook, covered, over low heat until the eggplant is soft and the tomato mixture is combined thoroughly, about 10 to 15 minutes. Meanwhile, cook the pasta according to package directions, omitting any oil and salt. Drain. Mix the pasta into the eggplant mixture and serve.

Makes 4 to 6 servings

Nutritional information per serving

Calories	276	Cal. from Fat (%)	4.6	Sodium (g)	182
Fat (g)	1.4	Saturated Fat (g)	0.2	Cholesterol (mg)	0
Protein (g)	10	Carbohydrate (g)	56.3		

Creamy Stuffed Zucchini

These zucchini boats are a fun way to eat zucchini, and the mild flavor will appeal to those who don't like a lot of seasoning. The sour cream makes it rich and creamy.

5 medium zucchini (about 2 pounds)
½ pound mushrooms, chopped
¼ cup all-purpose flour
½ teaspoon minced garlic

½ teaspoon dried oregano
Salt and pepper to taste
¼ cup nonfat sour cream
½ cup shredded reduced-fat Monterey Jack cheese

Cook the zucchini in boiling, salted water for 8 to 10 minutes, or until tender. Drain. Cut in half lengthwise. Remove the pulp and reserve, leaving a ¼-inch shell. Chop the pulp and place it in a skillet coated with nonstick cooking spray. Add the mushrooms, flour, garlic, oregano, and salt and pepper to the pulp, cooking over medium heat until the mushrooms are tender, about 5 minutes. Remove from the heat and carefully fold in the sour cream and Monterey Jack. Fill the zucchini shells with the mixture and place on a baking pan. Broil for 3 to 5 minutes, or until thoroughly heated and lightly browned.

Makes 6 servings

Nutritional information per serving

Calories	86	Cal. from Fat (%) 25.2		Sodium (g)	97
Fat (g)	2.4	Saturated Fat (g) 1.4		Cholesterol (mg)	8
Protein (g)	5.4	Carbohydrate (g) 12.1			

Fiesta Enchiladas

These light enchiladas are quite an attraction—you won't have to call your family to dinner twice.

1 (8-ounce) package part-
skim mozzarella cheese,
shredded, divided
1 (10-ounce) package frozen
chopped spinach, thawed
and squeezed dry
1 (10-ounce) package frozen
corn, thawed and drained

1 cup chopped onion
½ teaspoon minced garlic
Salt and pepper to taste
1 (15-ounce) container low-
fat ricotta cheese
1 large egg white
12 (8-inch) flour tortillas
1 (32-ounce) jar salsa

Preheat the oven to 375° F. In a mixing bowl, mix 1 cup of the mozzarella and the spinach, corn, onion, garlic, salt and pepper, ricotta, and egg white. Place ⅓ cup of the mixture evenly down the center of each tortilla. Roll the tortillas tightly and arrange them, seam side down, in a 3-quart casserole dish coated with nonstick cooking spray. Pour the salsa over the filled tortillas and sprinkle with the remaining mozzarella. Bake, covered, 50 minutes to 1 hour, or until the tortillas are heated through and the cheese is melted.

Makes 6 servings

Nutritional information per serving

Calories	628	Cal. from Fat (%)	23.8	Sodium (g)	1,961
Fat (g)	16.6	Saturated Fat (g)	7	Cholesterol (mg)	49
Protein (g)	33.2	Carbohydrate (g)	86.8		

Italian Eggplant Wedges

The bread crumbs that fall off the eggplant thicken the cooking liquid and make a great-tasting sauce to serve, too. This would also be great served over pasta.

1 large eggplant (2 to 2½ pounds)	¼ cup fat-free Italian dressing
1 onion, thinly sliced, rings cut in half	½ cup water
½ cup dry Italian bread crumbs	1 tomato, thinly sliced, slices cut in half
2 tablespoons Worcestershire sauce	½ cup shredded part-skim mozzarella cheese
	2 tablespoons dry red wine

Preheat the oven to 350° F. Peel the eggplant and trim off the ends. Cut lengthwise into 8 long wedges. Make a slit in each wedge ¼ inch wide, taking care not to go through the eggplant completely. Place the eggplant wedges in an 2-quart oblong baking dish coated with nonstick cooking spray. Place the onion slices between the slits. Pour the bread crumbs into the slit of each wedge, about 1 tablespoon each. Combine the Worcestershire sauce and Italian dressing. Drizzle the mixture on top of the eggplant. Pour the water over the top. Bake, covered, for 45 minutes. Remove from the oven, top the eggplant with the sliced tomato and mozzarella, and drizzle with the wine. Return to the oven and bake, uncovered, for 15 minutes longer.

Makes 2 to 4 servings

Nutritional information per serving

Calories	204	Cal. from Fat (%) 15.7		Sodium (g)	723
Fat (g)	3.6	Saturated Fat (g)	1.8	Cholesterol (mg)	8
Protein (g)	8.8	Carbohydrate (g)	35.4		

Tomatoes Stuffed with Wild Rice Salad ♥

The salad can be made ahead and the tomatoes scooped out and placed on a baking sheet to drain. Then simply fill the tomatoes with the salad before serving. If this sounds like too much trouble, don't skip this wonderful salad—just serve it on a bed of lettuce.

1 (6-ounce) package long-grain and wild rice
1 (10-ounce) package frozen peas, thawed
1 (15-ounce) can black beans, drained and rinsed
1 green bell pepper, seeded and chopped
1 bunch green onions (scallions), chopped

⅓ cup balsamic vinegar
1 teaspoon sugar
2 tablespoons lemon juice
¼ teaspoon paprika
½ teaspoon dry mustard
½ teaspoon minced garlic
10 medium-large tomatoes

Prepare the rice according to package directions, omitting any oil and salt. Let cool. In a large bowl, combine the cooked rice, peas, beans, green pepper, and green onions. In a small bowl, whisk together the vinegar, sugar, lemon juice, paprika, dry mustard, and garlic. Pour over the rice mixture, tossing well to coat. Meanwhile, cut the tops off the tomatoes and scoop out all the tomato pulp, carefully leaving the shell. Fill each tomato with the rice salad and serve.

Makes 8 to 10 servings

Nutritional information per serving

Calories	152	Cal. from Fat (%)	5.2	Sodium (g)	293
Fat (g)	0.9	Saturated Fat (g)	0.1	Cholesterol (mg)	0
Protein (g)	7.1	Carbohydrate (g)	31.2		

Veggie Rice with Feta ♥

This is a great way to use up the vegetables hanging around in the refrigerator. Toss with the feta for that added touch. If you have leftovers, serve cold as a salad the next day.

2 teaspoons minced garlic
1 cup chopped onion
1 cup chopped zucchini
1 cup broccoli florets, cut
   into small pieces
1 cup chopped yellow squash
½ cup chopped red bell
   pepper
1½ cups rice

3 cups canned fat-free
   chicken broth
1½ teaspoons dried oregano
1½ teaspoons dried basil
1½ teaspoons chili powder
¼ cup sliced pitted ripe
   black olives
⅓ cup crumbled feta cheese

In a large skillet coated with nonstick cooking spray, sauté the garlic, onion, zucchini, broccoli, squash, and red pepper over medium-high heat until tender, about 5 to 7 minutes. Add the rice and brown for 2 minutes, stirring constantly. Add the chicken broth, oregano, basil, chili powder, and olives. Bring to a boil, reduce the heat, cover, and cook for 20 to 30 minutes, or until the rice is tender. Toss with the feta and serve.

Makes 4 servings

Nutritional information per serving

Calories	384	Cal. from Fat (%)	11.9	Sodium (g)	673
Fat (g)	5.1	Saturated Fat (g)	2.5	Cholesterol (mg)	13
Protein (g)	11.6	Carbohydrate (g)	72		

Black-eyed Peas and Barley Pilaf ♥

Barley is a nice big, chewy grain and a good change from rice. Add black-eyed peas and you have a great vitamin- and protein-filled dish.

1 (10-ounce) package frozen peas	1 teaspoon dried thyme
½ cup medium barley	1 (15-ounce) can black-eyed peas, drained and rinsed
¼ cup chopped parsley	1 (14½-ounce) can vegetable broth
¼ cup chopped onion	

Combine the peas, barley, parsley, onion, thyme, black-eyed peas, and vegetable broth in a large saucepan and bring to a boil. Reduce the heat, cover, and simmer 15 to 20 minutes, or until the barley is tender and the liquid is absorbed.

Makes 4 servings

Nutritional information per serving

Calories	266	Cal. from Fat (%)	3.5	Sodium (g)	662
Fat (g)	1	Saturated Fat (g)	0.7	Cholesterol (mg)	0
Protein (g)	11.2	Carbohydrate (g)	53.1		

Fabulous Four-Bean Dish

The barbecue sauce and the assortment of beans makes this dish absolutely wonderful and it will attract those nonvegetarians, too.

1 cup rice
1 green bell pepper, seeded and thinly sliced
1 red bell pepper, seeded and thinly sliced
1 onion, chopped
1 (15-ounce) can black beans, drained and rinsed
1 (15-ounce) can red kidney beans, drained and rinsed

1 (15-ounce) can garbanzo beans, drained and rinsed
1 (15-ounce) can pinto beans, drained and rinsed
1 (10-ounce) can diced tomatoes and green chilies, with their juices
½ cup bottled barbecue sauce
1 cup water (optional)

Prepare the rice according to package directions, omitting any oil and salt. Meanwhile, in a skillet coated with nonstick cooking spray, sauté the green and red peppers and onion over medium heat until tender, about 5 minutes. Add the black beans, kidney beans, garbanzo beans, pink beans, tomatoes, and barbecue sauce to the pepper mixture in the skillet. Bring the mixture to a boil, reduce the heat, cover, and simmer 15 minutes. If the mixture is too thick, add the water as needed. To serve, place the bean mixture in a large platter, make a well in the center, and turn the rice out into the well.

Makes 5 servings

Nutritional information per serving

Calories	523	Cal. from Fat (%)	5.7	Sodium (g)	988
Fat (g)	3.3	Saturated Fat (g)	0.5	Cholesterol (mg)	0
Protein (g)	24.9	Carbohydrate (g)	100.1		

Eggplant Enchiladas ♥

The eggplant filling in these enchiladas produces a Mexican dish full of excitement.

1 cup chopped onion
½ teaspoon minced garlic
6 cups cubed peeled eggplant (about 2 small)
1 green bell pepper, seeded and chopped
1 cup sliced mushrooms
1 tablespoon Worcestershire sauce
Salt and pepper to taste
⅓ cup fat-free canned chicken broth
10 (10-inch) flour tortillas
1¼ cups shredded reduced-fat Monterey Jack cheese, divided
1 (14-ounce) can enchilada sauce
1 tablespoon minced parsley

Preheat the oven to 350° F. In a large skillet coated with nonstick cooking spray, sauté the onion and garlic over medium heat for 3 minutes. Stir in the eggplant, green pepper, mushrooms, and Worcestershire sauce. Cook, stirring, for 10 to 12 minutes, or until the eggplant is soft. Remove from the heat, add salt and pepper, and set aside. Simmer the vegetable broth in a small frying pan. Dip the tortillas in individually on each side to soften. Set aside ½ cup of the Monterey Jack. Put a portion of the eggplant mixture (about ¼ cup) and cheese (about 1 tablespoon) in each tortilla and roll tightly. Place the filled tortillas, seam side down, in a glass baking dish coated with nonstick cooking spray. Top the stuffed tortillas with the enchilada sauce and the remaining ¼ cup cheese and sprinkle with the parsley. Bake, uncovered, for 20 minutes.

Makes 10 enchiladas

Nutritional information per serving

Calories	201	Cal. from Fat (%)	30	Sodium (g)	452
Fat (g)	6.7	Saturated Fat (g)	2.4	Cholesterol (mg)	10
Protein (g)	7.5	Carbohydrate (g)	28.7		

Eggplant with Couscous Stuffing ♥

This unusual dish will get your family's attention. The feta, golden raisins, and couscous give it an Indian flair.

2 medium eggplant (1 to
  1½ pounds each), halved
  lengthwise
1½ cups couscous
1 (15-ounce) can garbanzo
  beans, drained and rinsed

1 cup chopped tomatoes
1 cup plain nonfat yogurt
¼ cup crumbled feta cheese
½ cup golden raisins
½ teaspoon dried basil
Salt and pepper to taste

Preheat the oven to 400° F. Prick the eggplant skins with a fork, then wrap each half in foil. Place on a baking sheet and bake for 30 to 35 minutes, or until soft; let cool until easy to handle. Meanwhile, prepare the couscous according to the package directions. Mix the couscous, garbanzos, tomatoes, yogurt, feta, raisins, basil, and salt and pepper in a large bowl. With a spoon, gently scoop out the eggplant flesh, leaving the shells and a ¼ inch of the pulp intact. Chop the flesh coarsely and stir into the couscous mixture. Mound the mixture into the eggplant shells. Arrange the stuffed eggplant on an ungreased 13 × 9 × 2-inch baking pan and bake, uncovered, for 15 minutes, or until well heated.

Makes 4 servings

Nutritional information per serving

Calories	539	Cal. from Fat (%)	10.3	Sodium (g)	401
Fat (g)	6.1	Saturated Fat (g)	2.6	Cholesterol (mg)	14
Protein (g)	22.1	Carbohydrate (g)	103		

DESSERTS

Loaded Brownies

I know you'll think these are too easy, too rich, and too good to be low-fat. Everyone of all ages will be reaching for these brownies.

1 (1-pound 3.8-ounce)
package low-fat brownie
cake mix
1 (10-ounce) package
miniature marshmallows

½ pound caramels
¼ cup evaporated skimmed
milk
Chocolate Topping (recipe
follows)

Preheat the oven to 350° F. Prepare the brownies according to package directions and pour into a 13 × 9 × 2-inch baking pan coated with nonstick cooking spray and dusted with flour. Bake for 20 to 25 minutes. Do not overcook. When done, top with the marshmallows and return to the oven for 3 to 5 minutes longer, or until the marshmallows are soft. Watch carefully. In a small microwaveproof bowl, heat the caramels and the evaporated milk in the microwave for 1 minute; stir, and heat for 1 minute longer, or until the mixture is smooth. Drizzle the caramel mixture over the marshmallows. Drizzle with the warm Chocolate Topping.

Makes 24 squares

Chocolate Topping

½ cup sugar
⅓ cup cocoa
1½ tablespoons cornstarch

⅔ cup skim milk
1 teaspoon vanilla extract

In a small saucepan, combine the sugar, cocoa, and cornstarch. Gradually add the milk, stirring until well blended. Bring this mixture to a boil over medium heat and cook for 1 minute, stirring constantly. Remove from the heat and add the vanilla.

Nutritional information per serving					
Calories	194	Cal. from Fat (%)	13	Sodium (g)	116
Fat (g)	2.8	Saturated Fat (g)	1.1	Cholesterol (mg)	0.9
Protein (g)	2.8	Carbohydrate (g)	41.8		

Marbled Brownies

The cream cheese in these brownies gives them a lighter chocolate flavor. If you enjoy cheesecake, this good-looking brownie will be high on your list.

6 tablespoons light stick
   margarine, softened
1 cup sugar, divided
1 large egg
2 large egg whites, divided

½ cup all-purpose flour
¼ cup cocoa
1 tablespoon vanilla extract
1 (8-ounce) package fat-free
   cream cheese, softened

Preheat the oven to 350° F. Coat a 9-inch square baking pan with nonstick cooking spray and dust with flour. In a large mixing bowl, beat the margarine and ¾ cup of the sugar until creamy. Add the egg and 1 egg white, blending well. In a measuring cup, combine the flour and cocoa. Gradually add the flour mixture to the margarine mixture. Add the vanilla. In another mixing bowl, combine the cream cheese and remaining sugar until creamy. Add the remaining egg white and continue to beat until well mixed. Pour two-thirds of the chocolate batter into the bottom of the baking pan. Spread the cream cheese batter over, and then spread with the remaining chocolate batter. Using a table knife, swirl it through the batter, making a marbleized effect. Bake for 30 minutes, or until the top of the brownie springs back when touched. Let cool for 20 minutes on a wire rack before cutting to give the cream cheese time to set.

Makes 20 to 25 brownies

Nutritional information per serving

Calories	72	Cal. from Fat (%)	28.2	Sodium (g)	80
Fat (g)	2.3	Saturated Fat (g)	0.5	Cholesterol (mg)	9
Protein (g)	2.3	Carbohydrate (g)	11.1		

Chocolate Chip Pie

This crustless pie is like eating a thick chocolate chip cookie. Heat and serve with frozen vanilla yogurt for a real treat.

2 cups all-purpose flour	1 large egg
1 tablespoon baking powder	1 large egg white
1½ cups light brown sugar	1 tablespoon vanilla extract
½ cup light stick margarine, melted	1 cup reduced-fat semisweet chocolate chips

Preheat the oven to 350° F. Combine the flour, baking powder, and brown sugar in a medium mixing bowl. Add the margarine, egg, egg white, and vanilla; stir well. Stir in the chocolate chips. Spoon into a 9-inch pie plate coated with nonstick cooking spray. Bake for 30 minutes, or until a knife inserted in the center comes out clean. Let cool on a wire rack.

Makes 8 servings

Nutritional information per serving

Calories	440	Cal. from Fat (%) 28.4	Sodium (g)	334
Fat (g)	13.9	Saturated Fat (g) 6.7	Cholesterol (mg)	27
Protein (g)	5.7	Carbohydrate (g) 78.7		

Pineapple Upside-Down Cake

Pineapple upside-down cake is as much a presentation as a delight to eat. This is a very light cake.

4 tablespoons (½ stick) light stick margarine	1 teaspoon grated orange rind
½ cup light brown sugar	¾ cup sugar
1 (20-ounce) can pineapple chunks, drained, juice reserved	1 teaspoon vanilla extract
	1 teaspoon imitation butter flavoring
1¼ cups all-purpose flour	2 large egg whites
1 teaspoon baking powder	

Place a rack on the lowest level of the oven and preheat the oven to 325° F. Melt the margarine in a 9-inch square baking pan in the oven. Sprinkle the brown sugar evenly over the bottom of the pan. Top the sugar with the pineapple chunks. Combine the flour, baking powder, orange rind, and sugar in a mixing bowl. In another mixing bowl, combine ½ cup of the reserved pineapple juice and the vanilla and butter flavoring and stir in the dry ingredients. In another mixing bowl, beat the egg whites until stiff peaks form. Fold into the batter. Pour the batter over the pineapple chunks in the pan. Bake for 40 to 45 minutes, or until a toothpick inserted in the center comes out clean. Let the cake cool in the pan for 10 minutes before inverting on a serving plate.

Makes 9 to 12 servings

Nutritional information per serving

Calories	186	Cal. from Fat (%) 13.7	Sodium (g)	94
Fat (g)	2.8	Saturated Fat (g) 0.5	Cholesterol (mg)	0
Protein (g)	2.1	Carbohydrate (g) 39		

Apricot Sponge Cake

As the cake soaks up the glaze, it becomes very moist and so good!

1 (18¼-ounce) package light white cake mix
1 (12-ounce) can apricot nectar, divided
1 (16-ounce) can light apricot halves, drained and finely chopped
1 large egg
3 large egg whites
⅓ cup canola oil
1 teaspoon vanilla extract
1⅓ cups confectioners' sugar

Preheat the oven to 350° F. In a mixing bowl, combine the cake mix, 1 cup of the apricot nectar, and the apricots, egg, egg whites, oil, and vanilla, mixing until smooth. Pour the batter into a 12-inch bundt pan coated with nonstick cooking spray and dusted lightly with flour. Bake for 40 to 45 minutes, or until a toothpick inserted in the center comes out clean. Invert onto a serving platter. In a microwaveproof dish, combine the confectioners' sugar and remaining nectar. Microwave on high for 60 to 90 seconds, or until the sugar is dissolved. Gradually pour the glaze over the warm cake.

Makes 16 servings

Nutritional information per serving

Calories	236	Cal. from Fat (%) 26	Sodium (g)	234
Fat (g)	6.8	Saturated Fat (g) 1.2	Cholesterol (mg)	13
Protein (g)	2.8	Carbohydrate (g) 41.6		

Apricot Crumble Squares

The thin cream cheese layer makes this the ultimate apricot square.

1 (18¼-ounce) package light yellow cake mix
½ cup light stick margarine, melted
1 (16-ounce) jar apricot preserves, divided
1 (8-ounce) package fat-free cream cheese, softened

¼ cup sugar
2 tablespoons all-purpose flour
1 large egg
1 teaspoon vanilla extract
¼ cup finely chopped almonds

Preheat the oven to 350° F. Coat a 13 × 9 × 2-inch pan with nonstick cooking spray and dust with flour. Combine the yellow cake mix and margarine in a large mixing bowl and beat at low speed with an electric mixer until crumbly. Reserve 1 cup of the crumb mixture. Press the remaining crumb mixture into the prepared pan. Carefully spread the preserves, reserving ⅓ cup, over the crumb mixture, leaving a ¼-inch border. In another mixing bowl, beat the cream cheese until smooth; add the reserved preserves and the sugar, flour, egg, and vanilla, beating well. Carefully spread the cream cheese mixture over the top of the preserves. Add the almonds to the reserved crumbs and sprinkle over the cream cheese mixture. Bake for 30 minutes, or until the top is golden brown and the center is set. Let cool completely in the pan on a wire rack. Cut into squares and refrigerate.

Makes 48 squares

Nutritional information per serving

Calories	91	Cal. from Fat (%)	21.9	Sodium (g)	116
Fat (g)	2.2	Saturated Fat (g)	0.6	Cholesterol (mg)	5
Protein (g)	1.3	Carbohydrate (g)	16.8		

Quickie Italian Cream Cake

Outstanding! This is too good and too easy to be true.

1 (18¼-ounce) package light
  white cake mix
1 cup low-fat buttermilk
2 large egg whites
1 large egg
¼ cup canola oil
3 tablespoons light brown
  sugar

¼ cup flaked coconut
2 tablespoons chopped
  pecans
Cream Cheese Frosting
  (recipe follows)

Preheat the oven to 350° F. Coat a 13 × 9 × 2-inch pan with nonstick cooking spray and dust with flour. In a large mixing bowl, combine the cake mix, buttermilk, egg whites, egg, and oil, beating until well mixed. In a small mixing bowl, combine the brown sugar, coconut, and pecans together; set aside. Spread half the batter in the bottom of the pan, sprinkle with the brown sugar mixture, and carefully top with the remaining batter, spreading it out. Bake for 30 minutes, or until a toothpick inserted in the center comes out clean. Let cool and spread with the Cream Cheese Frosting.

Makes 28 servings

Cream Cheese Frosting

1 (8-ounce) package fat-free
  cream cheese, softened
2 tablespoons light stick
  margarine

1 (16-ounce) box
  confectioners' sugar
1 teaspoon vanilla extract

In a mixing bowl, beat the cream cheese and margarine together. Blend in the sugar, mixing well. Add the vanilla, mixing well again.

Nutritional information per serving

Calories	185	Cal. from Fat (%)	21.5	Sodium (g)	190
Fat (g)	4.4	Saturated Fat (g)	1	Cholesterol (mg)	9
Protein (g)	2.8	Carbohydrate (g)	34		

Peach Almond Dump Cake

This simple cake satisfied my sister's sweet tooth one night. The name "dump cake" comes from the fact that you just dump a few ingredients into a bowl and end up with a scrumptious cake like this one.

1 (18¼-ounce) package light white cake mix
1½ cups water
3 large egg whites

2 teaspoons almond extract, divided
1 (21-ounce) can peach pie filling

Preheat the oven to 350° F. Coat a 13 × 9 × 2-inch baking pan with nonstick cooking spray and dust with flour. In a medium mixing bowl, prepare the cake mix according to package directions, using the water and egg whites. Add 1 teaspoon almond extract. Pour half the batter into the prepared pan. Stir the remaining almond extract into the pie filling and spread on top of the batter. Spread the remaining half of the batter to cover the filling. Bake for 30 to 35 minutes, or until a toothpick inserted in center comes out clean.

Makes 24 squares

Nutritional information per serving

Calories	107	Cal. from Fat (%) 10.8		Sodium (g)	154
Fat (g)	1.3	Saturated Fat (g) 0.5		Cholesterol (mg)	0
Protein (g)	1.5	Carbohydrate (g) 22.6			

Chocolate Black Forest Upside-Down Cake ♥

The oohs and ahs you'll receive when you serve this showy cake will make you feel like a million bucks. The rich dark chocolate and luscious cherry topping make it hard to pass up.

1 (21-ounce) can cherry pie filling
2¼ cups all-purpose flour
1½ cups sugar
¾ cup cocoa

1½ teaspoons baking soda
1½ cups water
⅓ cup canola oil
¼ cup vinegar
1½ teaspoons vanilla extract

Preheat the oven to 350° F. Spread the cherry pie filling on the bottom of a 13 × 9 × 2-inch pan. In a mixing bowl, combine the flour, sugar, cocoa, and baking soda; set aside. In another mixing bowl, combine the water, oil, vinegar, and vanilla. Add the liquid ingredients to the flour mixture all at once, stirring just enough to moisten the mixture. Pour the batter over the cherry pie filling. Bake for 45 to 50 minutes. Let cool 10 minutes, then invert onto a platter and let cool completely.

Makes 32 squares

Nutritional information per serving

Calories	116	Cal. from Fat (%) 20.5		Sodium (g)	66
Fat (g)	2.6	Saturated Fat (g) 0.3		Cholesterol (mg)	0
Protein (g)	1.3	Carbohydrate (g) 22.7			

German Chocolate Cake

No one, but no one will believe this is low-fat. Not only is it fabulous, it also serves a lot of people.

1 (18¼-ounce) package
  German chocolate cake
  mix
3 large egg whites
1¾ cups water
1 (14-ounce) can fat-free
  sweetened condensed milk
¼ cup flaked coconut

¼ cup chopped pecans
¼ cup light stick margarine,
  softened
⅓ cup cocoa
1 (16-ounce) box
  confectioners' sugar
1 teaspoon vanilla extract
3 to 4 tablespoons skim milk

Preheat the oven to 350° F. Coat a 15 × 11 × 1-inch baking pan with nonstick cooking spray and dust with flour. In a mixing bowl, beat together the cake mix, egg whites, and water for 3 minutes. Pour the batter into the prepared pan and bake for 15 minutes. Meanwhile, in a small bowl, combine the condensed milk, coconut, and pecans. Preheat the broiler. Pour this mixture over the top of the cake, spreading it evenly. Broil in the oven for about 2 minutes, until golden. Watch carefully. Remove from the oven and let cool. In a mixing bowl, beat together the margarine, cocoa, confectioners' sugar, and vanilla, adding the milk gradually until the frosting reaches spreading consistency. Spread over the cake.

Makes 48 squares

Nutritional information per serving

Calories	120	Cal. from Fat (%) 19.8		Sodium (g)	93
Fat (g)	2.6	Saturated Fat (g) 0.9		Cholesterol (mg)	1
Protein (g)	1.5	Carbohydrate (g) 23.6			

Blueberry Poppyseed Cake

This is like a blueberry pie with a shortbread crust. The tart lemon flavor with the sweet blueberries is the perfect combination. This would also be great with a scoop of frozen yogurt.

1 cup sugar, divided
6 tablespoons light stick margarine, softened
1 tablespoon grated lemon rind
1 large egg
1½ cups plus 1 tablespoon all-purpose flour, divided
1 tablespoon poppyseeds

½ teaspoon baking soda
½ cup nonfat sour cream
2 cups fresh blueberries, or 2 cups frozen blueberries, thawed and well drained
⅓ cup confectioners' sugar
1 tablespoon lemon juice, approximately

Preheat the oven to 350° F. Coat a 9- or 10-inch springform pan with nonstick cooking spray and dust with flour. In a mixing bowl, beat ⅔ cup of the sugar with the margarine until light and fluffy. Add the lemon rind and the egg, beating for 2 minutes. In another bowl, combine 1½ cups flour, poppyseeds, and baking soda; add to the margarine mixture alternately with the sour cream. Spread the batter over the bottom and 1 inch up the sides of the prepared pan. In a medium bowl, combine the drained blueberries, remaining sugar, and remaining flour, mixing gently. Spoon the blueberry mixture over the batter. Bake for 50 to 60 minutes, or until the crust is golden brown. Let cool slightly and remove the sides of the spring-form pan. In a cup, combine the confectioners' sugar and enough lemon juice to form a glaze of the desired consistency. Drizzle over the top of the warm cake.

Makes 12 servings

Nutritional information per serving

Calories	206	Cal. from Fat (%)	21.9	Sodium (g)	133
Fat (g)	5	Saturated Fat (g)	0.9	Cholesterol (mg)	19
Protein (g)	2.8	Carbohydrate (g)	37.9		

Cherry Oatmeal Cake

Oatmeal keeps this cake moist. If you're in a hurry, you can always substitute canned cherry pie filling, but this homemade version is so easy and good.

1¼ cups boiling water	2 large egg whites
1 cup old-fashioned oatmeal	1½ cups all-purpose flour
½ cup light stick margarine,	1 teaspoon baking soda
softened	1 teaspoon ground cinnamon
1½ cups sugar, divided	¼ cup cornstarch
1 cup light brown sugar	2 (16-ounce) cans pitted tart
1 teaspoon vanilla extract	red cherries, drained
1 large egg	

Preheat the oven to 350° F. Pour the boiling water over the oatmeal and let stand 20 minutes, stirring occasionally. In a mixing bowl, cream the margarine with ½ cup of the sugar and the brown sugar until smooth. Add the vanilla. Beat in the egg and egg whites, one at a time. Stir in the oatmeal, flour, baking soda, and cinnamon. Pour into a 9-inch square pan coated with nonstick cooking spray and dusted with flour. Bake for 40 to 45 minutes, or until a toothpick inserted in the center comes out clean. Meanwhile, in a medium saucepan, combine the remaining 1 cup sugar and the cornstarch. Add the cherries and cook, stirring constantly, until the mixture boils and thickens, about 5 to 7 minutes. Spread the cherry topping over the cake. Refrigerate any leftovers.

Makes 16 servings

Nutritional information per serving

Calories	257	Cal. from Fat (%)	16.8	Sodium (g)	160
Fat (g)	4.8	Saturated Fat (g)	0.9	Cholesterol (mg)	13
Protein (g)	3.3	Carbohydrate (g)	51.5		

Easy Mocha Cake

This chocolate cake is laced with a moist mocha filling. Serve warm with fat-free frozen vanilla yogurt for an amazing dessert.

1 (18¼-ounce) package light devil's food cake mix
1⅓ cups water
2 large eggs
2 large egg whites

½ cup light brown sugar
¼ cup sugar
¼ cup cocoa
1 cup strong cold coffee

Preheat the oven to 350° F. Prepare the cake mix with the water, eggs, and egg whites according to package directions and pour into a 13 × 9 × 2-inch baking pan coated with nonstick cooking spray and dusted with flour. In a small bowl, combine the brown sugar, sugar, cocoa, and coffee together and pour over the top of the cake. Bake for 35 minutes.

Makes 24 squares

Nutritional information per serving

Calories	122	Cal. from Fat (%)	13.1	Sodium (g)	170
Fat (g)	1.8	Saturated Fat (g)	0.8	Cholesterol (mg)	18
Protein (g)	1.8	Carbohydrate (g)	24.6		

Chocolate Banana Crumb Cake ♥

Chocolate and banana give this fabulous cake extra moistness. With the mix, it is very easy and a great opportunity to use up those over-ripe bananas.

1 cup old-fashioned oatmeal
½ cup light brown sugar
3 tablespoons light stick
   margarine, chilled and cut
   into pieces
2 teaspoons vanilla extract,
   divided
1 (18¼-ounce) package light
   devil's food cake mix

1¼ cups mashed very ripe
   bananas (about 3)
1 large egg
2 large egg whites
½ cup reduced-fat
   semisweet chocolate chips

Preheat the oven to 350° F. Coat a 13 × 9 × 2-inch baking pan with nonstick cooking spray and dust with flour. For the topping, combine the oatmeal and brown sugar in small bowl. Cut in the margarine until the mixture is crumbly. Stir in 1 teaspoon of the vanilla and set aside. In a large mixing bowl, combine the cake mix, bananas, egg, egg whites, and the remaining vanilla. Blend with a mixer at low speed until well mixed and continue beating for 2 minutes. Spread the batter in the baking pan. Sprinkle the top with the chocolate chips and oatmeal mixture. Bake for 35 minutes, or until a toothpick inserted in the center comes out clean.

Makes 24 servings

Nutritional information per serving

Calories	159	Cal. from Fat (%) 21.4		Sodium (g)	182
Fat (g)	3.8	Saturated Fat (g) 1.6		Cholesterol (mg)	9
Protein (g)	2.2	Carbohydrate (g) 29.2			

Banana Pudding Surprise

There's nothing like old-fashioned banana pudding, and the jam provides a sweet surprise. Use whatever flavor jam you have at home. This is best eaten on the same day it is made.

½ cup sugar
3 tablespoons cornstarch
2 cups skim milk
1 large egg yolk
1 teaspoon vanilla extract

30 low-fat vanilla wafers
2 ripe bananas, sliced
2 tablespoons strawberry
  jam

Combine the sugar and cornstarch in a heavy saucepan; stir well. Whisk together the milk and egg yolk in a mixing bowl. Gradually add the milk-egg mixture to the sugar and cornstarch in the saucepan. Bring to a boil over medium-low heat and cook 1 minute, stirring constantly. Remove from the heat. Stir in the vanilla. Spoon ¼ cup of the pudding mixture along the bottom of a 9×9×2-inch pan. Arrange half of the vanilla wafers on top of the pudding. Top each wafer with a banana slice. Spread half of the remaining pudding on top. Spread carefully with the jam and then layer with the remaining wafers. Top each wafer again with a banana slice. Cover with the remaining pudding and serve immediately or refrigerate.

Makes 6 servings

Nutritional information per serving

Calories	259	Cal. from Fat (%)	14.7	Sodium (g)	109
Fat (g)	4.2	Saturated Fat (g)	1.1	Cholesterol (mg)	49
Protein (g)	4.7	Carbohydrate (g)	52.2		

Cream Cheese Bread Pudding

Bread pudding is always a popular dessert, but with the cream cheese topping it reaches new heights!

1 (16-ounce) loaf French bread	1 teaspoon imitation butter flavoring
2 large eggs, divided	3 cups skim milk
4 large egg whites, divided	1 teaspoon ground cinnamon
1 cup sugar, divided	1 (8-ounce) package fat-free
1 teaspoon vanilla extract	cream cheese, softened

Preheat the oven to 350°F. Cut the French bread into 1-inch squares. Place the bread in a 13 × 9 × 2-inch baking dish. In a large bowl, lightly beat together 1 egg and 3 egg whites. Add ½ cup of the sugar, the vanilla, and the butter flavoring; mix well. Slowly add the milk to the egg mixture, mixing well. Pour over the bread squares. Sprinkle the mixture with the cinnamon. In a large mixing bowl, beat the cream cheese with the remaining sugar. Add the remaining egg and egg white, blending until smooth. Spread the mixture evenly over the soaked bread. Bake, uncovered, for 45 minutes, or until firm. Let cool slightly.

Makes 8 servings

Nutritional information per serving

Calories	340	Cal. from Fat (%)	8.3	Sodium (g)	573
Fat (g)	3.1	Saturated Fat (g)	0.9	Cholesterol (mg)	58
Protein (g)	15.5	Carbohydrate (g)	61.4		

Chocolate Trifle

A dazzling series of chocolate layers no one can resist. When you need a show-stopping quick dessert to serve a crowd, here's your answer. If you don't have a trifle bowl, you can use a large glass bowl.

1 (1-pound 2¼-ounce) package light devil's food cake mix
1⅓ cups water
1 large egg
2 large egg whites
1 (3.4 ounce) package instant chocolate pudding

3 cups cold skim milk
⅓ cup coffee liqueur
½ cup (two 1.4-ounce bars) chopped chocolate-covered toffee candy bars
1 (8-ounce) container frozen light whipped topping

Preheat the oven to 350° F. Coat two 9-inch round baking pans with nonstick cooking spray and dust with flour. Combine the cake mix, water, egg, and egg whites in a mixing bowl and beat for 2 minutes. Pour the batter evenly into the prepared pans. Bake for 25 to 30 minutes, or until a toothpick inserted in the center comes out clean. Let cool on a rack and then remove from the pans. In a mixing bowl, combine the pudding mix and milk and prepare according to package directions. Chill in the refrigerator. To assemble, place a cake layer in the bottom of a trifle dish, then sprinkle with half of the coffee liqueur, half of the toffee candy bars, half of the pudding, and half of the whipped topping. Repeat the layers.

Makes 16 servings

Nutritional information per serving

Calories	263	Cal. from Fat (%)	26.4	Sodium (g)	423
Fat (g)	7.7	Saturated Fat (g)	4.7	Cholesterol (mg)	17
Protein (g)	4.1	Carbohydrate (g)	45.3		

Lemon Pineapple Trifle

When tart lemon custard is combined with the pineapple-lemon filling, lemon lovers will not be able to contain themselves. This is a beautiful A+ dessert and will convert even the chocoholics!

¼ cup cornstarch
1 cup sugar
⅓ cup cold water
1 cup hot water
⅔ cup lemon juice
1 large egg yolk, lightly
  beaten
4 ounces fat-free cream
  cheese, softened

1 (8-ounce) can crushed
  pineapple, drained
1 (8-ounce) container frozen
  light whipped topping,
  thawed, divided
24 ladyfingers

In a medium saucepan, mix the cornstarch and sugar. Gradually add the cold water, stirring to mix. Add the hot water and lemon juice and bring to a boil over medium heat, stirring constantly. Cook until thickened and then gradually pour 1 cup of the hot mixture into the egg yolk in a small bowl, stirring constantly. Return that mixture to the custard and continue cooking for 1 minute. Transfer to a bowl, cover, and refrigerate until chilled. Divide the custard in half and mix half the custard with the cream cheese, mixing with a fork or whisk to blend. Mix in the pineapple. Fold half the container of whipped topping into the pineapple custard mixture; set aside. In a trifle bowl or a large glass bowl, place a layer of the ladyfingers along the bottom and around the side of the dish. Spread the bottom with half of the plain lemon custard. Spread with half of the pineapple-lemon filling. Top with the remaining ladyfingers. Spread with the remaining plain lemon custard and top with the rest of the pineapple-lemon filling. Top this with the remaining whipped topping. Refrigerate at least 2 hours before serving.

Makes 10 servings

Nutritional information per serving

Calories	269	Cal. from Fat (%) 19.4		Sodium (g)	99
Fat (g)	5.8	Saturated Fat (g)	3.7	Cholesterol (mg)	119
Protein (g)	4.9	Carbohydrate (g) 48.1			

Frozen Almond Yogurt Pie

Make this delicious, simply prepared pie ahead so it freezes up.

1 cup graham cracker
  crumbs
¼ cup chopped sliced
  almonds
2 tablespoons light stick
  margarine, melted
1 tablespoon water

2 teaspoons almond extract
1 quart frozen nonfat vanilla
  yogurt, softened slightly
1 (10-ounce) jar apricot
  preserves
½ cup sliced almonds, lightly
  toasted

Preheat the oven to 375° F. Combine the graham cracker crumbs, almonds, margarine, and water in a small mixing bowl and press into the bottom and up the sides of a 9-inch round pie plate coated with nonstick cooking spray. Bake for about 8 minutes, or until just lightly browned. Let cool completely. Stir the almond extract into the slightly softened yogurt and quickly spread over the cooled graham cracker crust. Cover with plastic wrap and freeze. Before serving, spread the pie with the preserves and top with the almonds. Freeze until just before serving.

Makes 8 to 10 servings

Nutritional information per serving

Calories	269	Cal. from Fat (%)	26	Sodium (g)	161
Fat (g)	7.8	Saturated Fat (g)	1	Cholesterol (mg)	3.2
Protein (g)	6.1	Carbohydrate (g)	46.4		

Peach and Blueberry Summer Spectacular

A store-bought angel food cake layered with cream cheese filling and fruit proves to be sensational!

1 (16-ounce) angel food cake
1 (8-ounce) package fat-free
  cream cheese, softened
½ cup confectioners' sugar
½ teaspoon vanilla extract
1 (8-ounce) container frozen
  light whipped topping,
  thawed

1 cup fresh blueberries
1 cup diced peeled fresh
  peaches
6 tablespoons almond
  liqueur, divided

Slice the angel food cake horizontally into three layers; set aside. Blend the cream cheese and confectioners' sugar until smooth. Add the vanilla. Fold in the whipped topping, mixing gently until well combined. In another bowl, mix together the blueberries and peaches. Place the bottom layer of the cake on a plate. Drizzle with 2 tablespoons of the almond liqueur. Spread a layer of the cream cheese mixture and top with half of the fruit. Top with the second cake layer, drizzle with another 2 tablespoons of the almond liqueur, spread with the cream cheese mixture, and top with the remaining fruit. Top this with the third cake layer and drizzle with the remaining almond liqueur. Frost the sides and top with the remaining cream cheese mixture. Refrigerate until ready to serve.

Makes 8 to 10 servings

Nutritional information per serving

Calories	268	Cal. from Fat (%) 11.1		Sodium (g)	451
Fat (g)	3.3	Saturated Fat (g) 2.9		Cholesterol (mg)	2
Protein (g)	6.1	Carbohydrate (g) 48.3			

Nectarine Crumble

Nectarines instead of peaches are the star of this yummy dessert!

4 cups sliced peeled nectarines
¼ cup plus ⅓ cup sugar, divided
1½ teaspoons grated lemon rind
1 tablespoon lemon juice

¼ teaspoon ground cinnamon
¼ teaspoon ground ginger
½ cup all-purpose flour
3 tablespoons light stick margarine, softened

Preheat the oven to 350° F. Place the nectarines in a shallow 1½-quart baking dish. Sprinkle with the ¼ cup sugar, rind, lemon juice, cinnamon, and ginger. Combine the remaining sugar, flour, and margarine in a bowl, mixing with a fork until crumbly. Sprinkle over the nectarines. Bake for 40 to 50 minutes, until lightly golden.

Makes 4 servings

Nutritional information per serving

Calories	291	Cal. from Fat (%) 21.1		Sodium (g)	92
Fat (g)	6.8	Saturated Fat (g) 1.2		Cholesterol (mg)	0
Protein (g)	2.0	Carbohydrate (g) 57.8			

Caramel Cheesecake

Cheesecake combined with caramel makes this a very popular variation on an old favorite. Remember, cheesecake freezes quite well, so it can be made ahead of time.

1 cup graham cracker crumbs
2 tablespoons granulated sugar
¼ cup light stick margarine, melted
2 (8-ounce) packages light cream cheese
1 (8-ounce) package fat-free cream cheese

1¼ cups light brown sugar
1 large egg
3 large egg whites
3 tablespoons all-purpose flour
1½ teaspoons vanilla extract
½ cup fat-free caramel topping

Preheat the oven to 350° F. Combine the graham cracker crumbs, granulated sugar, and margarine together in a small bowl. Press evenly into the bottom of a 9-inch springform pan. In a large mixing bowl, blend together the light cream cheese, fat-free cream cheese, and brown sugar until smooth. Add the egg and egg whites one at a time, beating well after each addition. Stir in the flour and vanilla. Reserve 1 cup of the batter and add the caramel topping to it, mixing well. Spoon half of the plain batter over the crust, cover with the caramel batter layer, and spread the remaining plain batter over the top. Bake for 55 minutes, or until set. Let the cheesecake cool to room temperature, cover, and refrigerate until well chilled at least 2 hours.

Makes 10 to 12 servings

Nutritional information per serving

Calories	311	Cal. from Fat (%)	29.5	Sodium (g)	437
Fat (g)	10.2	Saturated Fat (g)	4.6	Cholesterol (mg)	41
Protein (g)	9	Carbohydrate (g)	46		

RECIPE	EXCHANGE
All-American Egg Bake	1 very lean meat, 1 starch, 1 fat
Apricot Crumble Squares	0.5 starch, 0.5 fruit, 0.5 fat
Apricot Sponge Cake	1 starch, 2 fruit, 1 fat
Artichoke and Mushroom Fettuccine	3 starch, 3 vegetable, 1 fat
Baked Fish on Rice Pilaf	3 very lean meat, 2 starch, 0.5 fat
Baked French Toast	1.5 starch, 1 fat
Baked Stuffed Fish with Cheese Sauce	3.5 very lean meat, 2 vegetable, 1 low-fat milk
Baked Waffles and Ham	1 lean meat, 2 starch, 0.5 skim milk, 1 fat
Banana Pudding Surprise	2 starch, 1 fruit, 1 fat
Barbecue Burger and Bean Bake	2 lean meat, 3 starch
Beef and Salsa Fajitas	5 lean meat, 4 starch, 3 vegetable
Beefy Bow Ties	2 lean meat, 2 starch, 4 vegetable
Beefy Jamaican Stir-Fry	2 lean meat, 3 starch, 2 vegetable, 1 fat
Black-eyed Peas and Barley Pilaf	3.5 starch
Blueberry Pancakes	2 starch, 0.5 fat
Blueberry Poppyseed Cake	1 starch, 1.5 fruit, 1 fat
Breakfast Tortillas Santa Fe	1.5 lean meat, 2 starch, 1 vegetable, 1 fat
Broccoli Soup	1 very lean meat, 1 starch, 0.5 vegetable, 1 fat
Caramel Cheesecake	2 starch, 1 fruit, 2 fat
Cheesy Shrimp-Rice Casserole	3 very lean meat, 1 starch, 3 vegetable, 1 fat
Cherry Oatmeal Cake	1 starch, 2.5 fruit, 1 fat
Chicken and Artichoke Vermicelli	3.5 very lean meat, 3 starch, 2 vegetable, 0.5 fat
Chicken and Beef Shish Kabobs	5 very lean meat, 2 vegetable, 1.5 fat
Chicken and Broccoli Casserole	5 very lean meat, 1 starch, 2 vegetable, 1.5 fat
Chicken and Potatoes Picante	3 lean meat, 1 starch, 2 vegetable
Chicken Creole	6 very lean meat, 3 starch , 3 vegetable, 0.5 fat
Chicken Fiesta Salad	3 very lean meat, 2 starch, 1 fat
Chicken Florentine	5 very lean meat, 1 starch, 3 vegetable, 2 fat
Chicken Kiwi Salad	8 very lean meat, 6 vegetable, 1.5 fat
Chicken Oregano with Angel Hair	3 very lean meat, 2 starch, 1 vegetable, 1 fat
Chicken Peanut Pasta Salad	3 lean meat, 3 starch, 3 vegetable, 0.5 fat
Chicken Pot Pies	2 very lean meat, 1 starch, 3 vegetable, 1 fat
Chicken Rice Stir-Fry	3 very lean meat, 2 starch, 4 vegetable, 1 fat
Chicken Salad Olé	4 very lean meat, 1 starch, 2 vegetable, 1.5 fat
Chicken, Barley, and Bow-Tie Soup	3 very lean meat, 2 starch, 2 vegetable
Chicken, Broccoli, and Rice	3 lean meat, 4 starch, 3 vegetable
Chicken, Shrimp, and Sausage Gumbo	6 very lean meat, 3 starch, 4 vegetable, 1 fat
Chicken-Vegetable Stroganoff	3 very lean meat, 4 starch, 1 vegetable, 1 fat
Chili	3 very lean meat, 1 starch, 2 vegetable, 1 fat
Chinese Pork Vermicelli	3 very lean meat, 2 starch, 1 vegetable, 1 fat
Chocolate Banana Crumb Cake	1 starch, 1 fruit, 0.5 fat
Chocolate Black Forest Cake	0.5 starch, 1 fruit, 0.5 fat
Chocolate Chip Pie	2 starch, 3 fruit, 2 fat
Chocolate Trifle	3 fruit, 0.5 skim milk, 1 fat
Chunky Chicken Divan	5 very lean meat, 2 vegetable, 1.5 fat
Crabmeat and Artichoke Pasta Casserole	3.5 very lean meat, 3 starch, 5 vegetable, 2 fat
Crabmeat Au Gratin	3 lean meat, 1 starch
Cranberry Chicken with Wild Rice	4 very lean meat, 3 starch, 0.5 fruit
Crawfish and Rice Casserole	1 very lean meat, 1 starch, 2 vegetable, 1 fat
Crawfish Enchiladas	2 very lean meat, 3 starch, 3 vegetable, 1 fat
Crawfish Jambalaya	2 very lean meat, 2 starch
Cream Cheese Bread Pudding	0.5 very lean meat, 4 starch
Creamy Chicken and Spinach	3 very lean meat, 1 skim milk, 0.5 fat
Creamy Shrimp with Vermicelli	3 very lean meat, 3 starch, 0.5 fat
Creamy Stuffed Zucchini	2 vegetable, 0.5 fat

RECIPE	EXCHANGE
Creamy Tomato Pasta	1 very lean meat, 3 starch, 1 vegetable,
Crispy Chicken and Bean Burritos	2 lean meat, 2 starch, 4 vegetable, 1 fat
Crispy Southwestern Lasagne	3 lean meat, 2 starch, 1 vegetable
Crowd-Pleaser Pasta Salad	1 very lean meat, 2 starch, 2 vegetable
Crustless Spinach Mushroom Quiche	1 very lean meat, 2 vegetable, 0.5 fat
Curried Orzo Salad	8 starch, 1 vegetable, 1 fruit
Deli Pasta Salad	1 very lean meat, 3 starch, 2 vegetable
Different Twist Pork Stew	3 very lean meat, 3 starch, 2 vegetable, 1 fat
Easy Mocha Cake	1 starch, 0.5 fruit
Eggplant and Ziti	3 starch, 1 vegetable
Eggplant Enchiladas	1 starch, 3 vegetable, 1 fat
Eggplant with Couscous Stuffing	5 starch, 4 vegetable, 1 fat
Enchilada Casserole	2 lean meat, 2 starch, 1 fat
Fabulous Four-Bean Dish	5 starch, 4 vegetable, 0.5 fat
Fiesta Enchiladas	2 lean meat, 5 starch, 2 vegetable, 1.5 fat
Fish Florentine	5 very lean meat, 2 vegetable, 1 skim milk
Florentine English Muffins	1 starch, 1 vegetable, 0.5 fat
Frozen Almond Yogurt Pie	2 starch, 1 fruit, 1 fat
Garden Pasta	2.5 starch, 2 vegetable, 1 fat
Gazpacho with Shrimp	1 very lean meat, 2 vegetable
German Chocolate Cake	0.5 starch, 1 fruit, 0.5 fat
Ginger Chicken and Black Beans	5 very lean meat, 2 starch, 1 fat
Glazed Turkey with Cornbread Stuffing	6 very lean meat, 3 starch, 4 vegetable
Greek Chicken Salad Bowl	3 very lean meat, 2 vegetable, 1 fat
Greek Shrimp Orzo	2.5 very lean meat, 4 starch, 1 vegetable, 1 fat
Hearty Hamburger Meal	3 very lean meat, 4 starch, 2 vegetable, 1 fat
Herbed Shrimp and Pasta Casserole	2 lean meat, 3 starch
Hot Chicken Salad	4.5 very lean meat, 2 starch, 1 fat
Hot Potatoes	1 starch, 2 vegetable, 0.5 fat
Indian Chicken Salad	4 very lean meat, 1 starch, 2 vegetable, 1 fruit, 1 fat
Italian Chicken	5 very lean meat, 2 starch, 3 vegetable, 1 fat
Italian Eggplant Wedges	2 starch, 1 vegetable, 0.5 fat
Italian Eggplant, Meat, and Rice	2 lean meat, 1 starch, 3 vegetable
Italian Meaty Pasta Dish	3 lean meat, 3 starch
Italian Pork, Squash, and Tomatoes	3 very lean meat, 3 starch, 2 vegetable, 1.5 fat
Italian Scramble	2 very lean meat, 1 vegetable
Italian Vegetable and Meat Pasta	2 lean meat, 3 starch, 2 vegetable
Layered Pasta and Spinach Surprise	2 lean meat, 2 starch, 2.5 vegetable, 1 fat
Lemon Pineapple Trifle	1 very lean meat, 3 fruit, 1 fat
Loaded Brownies	1 starch, 2 fruit
Macaroni and Cheese Soup	1 very lean meat, 2 starch, 2 vegetable, 0.5 fat
Mandarin Chicken Salad	3.5 very lean meat, 1 vegetable, 1 fruit, 1 fat
Manicotti	2 very lean meat, 1 starch, 3 vegetable, 0.5 fat
Marbled Brownies	1 starch
Meat Sauce with Angel Hair Pasta	3 lean meat, 3 starch, 2 vegetable
Meatball Stew	4 very lean meat, 2 starch, 2 vegetable, 1 fat
Mediterranean Catch	4 very lean meat, 3 starch, 1 vegetable, 1.5 fat
Mexican Brunch Biscuit Bake	1 starch, 1.5 vegetable, 1 fat
Mexican Chicken Casserole	6 very lean meat, 2 starch, 2 vegetable, 2.5 fat
Mock Cabbage Rolls	2 lean meat, 2 starch, 3 vegetable, 1 fat
Mushroom Lasagne	1.5 lean meat, 1 starch, 1 vegetable
Nectarine Crumble	1 starch, 3 fruit, 1 fat
Old-Fashioned Beefy Vegetable Stew	3 lean meat, 2 starch, 3 vegetable

RECIPE	EXCHANGE
Old-Fashioned Pork Chop Casserole	2 lean meat, 2 starch, 1 fat
Orange-Glazed Cornish Hens with Rice Stuffing	6 very lean meat, 2 starch, 2 fat
Orange Roughy Florentine Fettuccine ...	3 very lean meat, 3 starch, 2 vegetable
Orzo Paella	5 very lean meat, 8 starch, 0.5 fat
Paella	3 very lean meat, 2 starch, 3 vegetable
Paella Salad	2 very lean meat, 2 starch, 4 vegetable
Pasta Tomato Soup Florentine	3 starch, 1 vegetable, 0.5 fat
Peach Almond Dump Cake	1 starch, 0.5 fruit
Peach and Blueberry Spectacular	2 starch, 1 fruit, 1 fat
Penne with Spinach, Sun-Dried Tomatoes, and Goat Cheese	1 lean meat, 4 starch, 1 vegetable, 3 fat
Pineapple Upside-Down Cake	1 starch, 2 fruit
Pizza-Baked Fish	4 very lean meat, 2 vegetable, 1 fat
Plentiful Pork Soup	2 very lean meat, 2 starch, 0.5 fat
Poached Salmon with Potato Salad	4 very lean meat, 2 starch, 1 vegetable, 1 fat
Polynesian Chicken	2 very lean meat, 5 starch, 3 vegetable, 1 fat
Pork and Wild Rice Stir-Fry	2 very lean meat, 2 starch, 1 vegetable, 0.5 fat
Pork Chop and Lima Bean Supper	3 very lean meat, 2 starch, 1 vegetable, 0.5 fat
Pork Southwestern Style	4 very lean meat, 3 starch, 1 vegetable, 1 fat
Pork Tenderloin Diane	6 lean meat, 2 starch
Quickie Italian Cream Cake	2 starch, 1 fat
Red Snapper Dill Divan	5 very lean meat, 2 vegetable, 1 fat
Rice Taco Salad	2 lean meat, 1 starch, 3 vegetable
Rich and Creamy Chicken and Potatoes ..	5 very lean meat, 3 starch, 1 fat
Roasted Eye of Round and Vegetables ...	5 very lean meat, 1 starch, 1.5 fat
Roasted Stuffed Chicken and Vegetables ..	5 very lean meat, 2 starch, 1 vegetable, 2 fat
Salmon Fettuccine	2 very lean meat, 3 starch, 3 vegetable, 1 fat
Salmon Pasta Salad	3 lean meat, 2 starch
Salsa Pasta Salad	4 starch, 1 vegetable
Scallops in Tarragon Sauce	2.5 very lean meat, 4 starch
Shrimp and Rice Florentine	2 lean meat, 2 starch, 2 vegetable
Shrimp and Chicken Étouffée	4 very lean meat, 3 starch, 1 vegetable
Shrimp and Corn Soup	2 very lean meat, 2 starch
Shrimp and Rice Salad	1 lean meat, 2 starch, 1 vegetable
Shrimp and Tomato Pasta	2.5 very lean meat, 3 starch
Shrimp Pasta Thai Time	3 very lean meat, 2 starch, 1 vegetable, 0.5 fat
Shrimp Rosemary and Pasta	2 very lean meat, 3 starch, 1 vegetable
Shrimp Stuffed Peppers	1 very lean meat, 2 starch
Shrimp with Dill	4 very lean meat, 2.5 starch, 1 fat
Shrimp with Oranges and Pasta	3.5 very lean meat, 4.5 starch, 1 fat
Shrimp with Potatoes	2 very lean meat, 2 starch
Shrimp, Peas, and Rice	1 lean meat, 3 starch
Shrimp, White Bean, and Pasta Soup	2 very lean meat, 2 starch
Shrimp Ziti Primavera	2 very lean meat, 3 starch, 2 vegetable
Simple Chicken Combo	2 very lean meat, 3 starch, 2 vegetable
Simply Spinach and Pasta	3 starch, 1.5 vegetable
Sirloin Strips with Mushroom Sauce	3 lean meat, 2 starch
Sloppy Joes	2 lean meat, 3 starch, 1 vegetable, 1 fat
Smoked Pork Chop Dinner	6 very lean meat, 2 starch, 1 fruit, 1 fat
Smoked Salmon and Ziti	1 lean meat, 3 starch
Smoked Turkey and Wild Rice Salad	1 very lean meat, 1 starch, 2 vegetable, 0.5 fat
Smothered Chicken	4 very lean meat, 2 starch, 1 vegetable, 1 fat
Snapper-Vegetable Gratin	3 very lean meat, 2 vegetable, 1 low-fat milk

RECIPE	EXCHANGE
Southwestern Chicken and Bean Salad . . .	5 very lean meat, 1 starch, 1 vegetable, 1 fat
Southwestern Fish	2 lean meat, 1 starch
Southwestern Pork Stew	3 very lean meat, 1 starch, 3 vegetable, 1 fat
Southwestern Pot Roast	7 very lean meat, 1 starch, 2 vegetables, 1 fat
Southwestern Shrimp and	
Angel Hair	1 lean meat, 3 starch
Southwestern Shrimp and	
Black Bean Chili	2 very lean meat, 1 starch, 2 vegetable
Southwestern Vegetable Soup	2 starch, 1 vegetable, 0.5 fat
Speedy Southwest Pasta Casserole	2 lean meat, 2 starch, 2 vegetable
Spicy Chicken Enchiladas	2 lean meat, 2 starch, 2 vegetable
Spicy Citrus Beef	3 lean meat, 2 vegetable, 1 fruit
Spicy Corn and Squash Chowder	2 starch, 3 vegetable
Spicy Pasta Salad	2 starch, 2 vegetable
Spinach Beef Casserole	3 lean meat, 1 starch, 2 vegetable
Spinach Chef Salad with Creamy Dressing	1 very lean meat, 1 starch
Spinach Manicotti	1 very lean meat, 1 starch, 2 vegetable, 0.5 fat
Spinach Roll-Ups	1 very lean meat, 2 starch, 1 vegetable, 0.5 fat
Squash, Tomato, and Bow-Tie Pasta	4 starch, 1 vegetable, 0.5 fat
Steak Creole with Cheese Grits	7 very lean meat, 2 starch, 2 fat
Stir-Fried Shrimp and Scallops	2 lean meat, 4 starch, 2 vegetables
Stuffed Pasta Peppers	2 starch, 3 vegetable, 0.5 fat
Sweet-and-Sour Chicken, Potatoes,	
and Spinach	4 very lean meat, 2 starch, 1 vegetable, 0.5 fat
Swiss Steak	4 very lean meat, 3 vegetable, 1 fat
Tamale Pie	2 lean meat, 1 starch, 1 vegetable
Tarragon Beef Stew	4 lean meat, 3 starch
Tarragon Chicken with Carrots	4 very lean meat, 2 starch, 2 vegetable, 1 fat
Tex-Mex Chicken Chowder	4 very lean meat, 1 starch, 1 vegetable, 1 fat
Tex-Mex Eggs	2 very lean meat, 1 starch, 1 fat
Tex-Mex Tuna Salad	4 very lean meat, 1 starch, 4 vegetable
Thai Pasta Dish	3 starch
Three-Bean Soup	1 very lean meat, 2 starch, 1 vegetable
Tomatoes Stuffed with Wild Rice Salad . .	2 starch
Tortilla Soup	2 very lean meat, 1 starch, 1 vegetable, 1 fat
Tropical Shrimp Salad	2 very lean meat, 2 starch, 2 fruit, 0.5 fat
Tropical Shrimp Salsa over Rice	3 very lean meat, 2 starch, 1 fruit
Tuna Macaroni Casserole	1.5 very lean meat, 3 starch
Tuna-Artichoke Pasta Salad	1 very lean meat, 2 starch, 2 vegetable
Tuna-Orzo Salad	2 lean meat, 5 starch, 3 vegetable
Turkey and Rice Bake	4 very lean meat, 3 starch, 1 vegetable
Two-Potato Bisque	1 starch, 1 vegetable
Veal and Tomatoes with Angel Hair	0.5 very lean meat, 3 starch, 2 vegetable, 1 fat
Veal Stew	3 lean meat, 3 starch, 2 vegetable
Veal, Mushroom, and Barley Soup	1 lean meat, 2 starch, 1 vegetable
Vegetable Medley Lasagne	1 very lean meat, 1 starch, 2 vegetable, 1 fat
Veggie Rice with Feta	4 starch, 2 vegetable, 1 fat
Vermicelli Feta Salad	1 lean meat, 3 starch, 1 vegetable, 1.5 fat
Vichyssoise	1 starch, 0.5 skim milk, 0.5 fat
Waldorf Pasta Salad	2 starch, 1 fruit, 1 fat
Western Breakfast Rice	2 starch, 2 vegetable, 1 fat
White Chicken Chili	3 very lean meat, 2 starch, 1 vegetable
Wild Rice and Pork Salad	2 lean meat, 3 starch, 1 fruit
Ziti Zucchini	2 starch, 3 vegetable
Zucchini Frittata	1 very lean meat, 2 vegetable, 0.5 fat

Index